Writing an Interpreter in Object Pascal:

Part 1: Lexical and Basic Syntax Analysis

Herbert M. Sauro
Seattle, WA

Ambrosius Publishing

Published by Ambrosius Publishing and Future Skill Software
books.analogmachine.org

Typeset using LATEX 2_ε, TikZ, PGFPlots, WinEdt
and 11pt Math Time Professional 2 Fonts

pgf version is: 3.0.1a

pgfplots version is 1.16

ISBN 10: 1-7325486-0-9 (paperback)
ISBN 13: 978-1-7325486-0-2 (paperback)

Printed in the United States of America.

Mosaic image modified from Daniel Steger's Tikz image (http://www.texample.net/tikz/examples/mosaic-from-pompeii/)

If you've purchased the printed copy you can get a 50% discount for the pdf version using the following code:

PDF Discount code: cambrian$

at https://gum.co/GbsgR

Contents

Preface

I've been writing interpreters on and off for many years. In all, I've written five interpreters, in straight Pascal, 2 × C, C# and Object Pascal. These were written to support various domain specific languages for my work. Given this background I thought it time to write a how-to book on interpreters using Object Pascal. I've decided to publish this material in at least two parts. The first will focus on lexical analysis and an introduction to syntax analysis. Part 2 will focus on code generation, the virtual machine, and developing an interactive console for the interpreter. I'm publishing the series in two parts because it's simply more practical in terms of the time I can allocate to the project. On a personal note, I've programmed substantial applications in C, and C# and smaller applications in C++, and Python and I manage a reasonably large C++ project.

As with all my books, I decided to publish this book myself. I have found that traditional publishers have yet to catch up with modern publishing trends, in particular, the loss of copyright on the text as well as any figures and even more problematic, the inability to rapidly update the text to correct errors or when new material needs to be added. Publishers still handle corrections via errata pages rather than updating the book itself. With today's print on demand technology, the restrictions imposed by publishers seem unnecessary.

There are many people and organizations whom I should thank, but foremost must be my infinitely patient wife, Holly, and my two boys Theodore and Tyler who have put up with the many hours I have spent working alone. I want to thank Holly in particular for helping me edit the text. I am also most grateful to the National Science Foundation and the National Institutes of Health who paid my summer salary so that I could allocate some time to write, edit and research. Naturally, I am responsible for the remaining errors. Or as a contributor (Marc Claesen) to StackOverflow once humorously remarked, 'Making the manuscript error-free is left as an exercise for the reader.'.

Many thanks to the authors of the TeX system, MikTeX (2.9), TikZ (3.0.1a), PGFPlots (1.16), WinEdt (10.2), Inkscape (0.48.4), and Createspace/KDP for making available such amazing tools for technical authors. It is these tools that make it possible for individuals like myself to publish. Finally, I should thank Michael Corral (http://www.mecmath.net/) and Mike Hucka (www.sbml.org) whose LaTeX work inspired some of the styles I used in the text.

All code can be obtained from: https://github.com/penavon/BookPart1

November 2018
Seattle, WA

HERBERT M. SAURO

Source Code

All source code is licensed under the open source license Apache 2.0.

http://www.apache.org/licenses/LICENSE-2.0

The source code can be obtained from GitHub at:

```
https://github.com/penavon/BookPart1
```

1

Introduction

THIS book was inspired by the textbook 'Writing an Interpreter in GO' by Thorsten Ball. The code you'll find in this book is entirely different, however, it is based on an older project I did some years ago. The spirit and sentiment are the same as Ball, with a similar objective, being a practical introduction to writing interpreters.

As Ball states in his introduction, there aren't any practical books on writing interpreters. Many of the existing books, which are mainly about writing compilers, are geared towards students or professionals in the industry who need a solid grounding in the theory of language interpretation and translation. What's missing are practical books for either curious users, those, who for one reason or another, would rather not delve too much into the theory, or someone who wants to quickly get up to speed and write a compiler or interpreter.

There are a number of books published describing how to write either a compiler or interpreter (usually a compiler). Some of the most well-known oldies include:

1. Peter John Brown (1979) Writing Interactive Compilers and Interpreters, Wiley

2. Payne and Payne (1982) Implementing BASICSs: How BASICSs Work, Reston Publishing

3. Brinch Hansen (1985) Brinch Hansen on Pascal Compilers, Prentice Hall

4. Ronald Mak (1991) Writing Compilers & Interpreters, An Applied Approach, Wiley

5. Niklaus Wirth (1996) Compiler Construction, Addison-Wesley

6. Grune et al. (2000) Modern Compiler Design. Wiley (Now with a second edition 2012, Springer)

If I had to prioritize the above list, I would probably recommend reading the first edition Mak. He describes in detail a Pascal-like compiler written in C. For whatever reason, I found his C code not difficult to understand. His subsequent editions use C++ and Java respectively, and I found those, more challenging.

Of the others, Brown focuses on writing a Basic interpreter and is one of the classic books for the hobbyist community from the 1970s. Likewise, the 1992 book by Payne and Payne delves into writing a Basic interpreter. Hansen's book uses Pascal to write a Pascal-like compiler with lots of useful information including a complete listing for the compiler in the appendix. Wirth describes in detail how to write a compiler using Oberon-0. Grune et al. is also recommended, though it's more on theory based but a fairly easy read. Of these, the bulk of them talk about writing compilers. In fact, the vast majority of published books are about compiler design. There are in fact, very few books on how to write an interpreter. Mak has some discussion on interpreters, but it's mainly a book on compiler writing. I'm not sure why there are far fewer books written on interpreters, especially given that many of us probably use interpreters every day in some form. Ball's book stands out as one of the few practical and recent books on writing interpreters.

I include a much longer list of books at the end of the chapter. Some of you might be curious (and shocked?) that I haven't mentioned the Dragon book[1]. This book is repeatedly recommended on forums like StackOverflow. However, it is very focused on theory, it's dense, and there is very little real code to illustrate ideas. I wouldn't recommend it as a first book to turn to, or even the second. I think the Dragon book is more useful when you've already had some experience and understand the basics, at which point a more thorough grounding in the theory can be quite useful.

Before moving on, I can't help but mention 'The Unix Programming Environment' by Brian W. Kernighan and Rob Pike (1983). What's interesting about this book is the appendix which describes the High Order Calculator, HOC. The development proceeds in stages, becoming more and more sophisticated. HOC uses the well-known parser generator Yacc (Yet another compiler compiler), but many of the ideas also apply to non-Yacc users. In case you're wondering, we won't be using compiler generators such as Yacc. A final favorite which I can't omit is the online text,[2] "Let's Build a Compiler" by Jack Crenshaw.[3]

1.1 What are we Going to Build?

In this book, we will focus on writing an interactive interpreter. I've been interested in writing interpreters for some time and have written five reasonably comprehensive interpreters

---

[1] Aho et al., Compilers Principles, Techniques and Tools, 1986, Addison-Wesley

[2] https://compilers.iecc.com/crenshaw/

[3] You'll find a LaTeXed version on my website: http://blog.analogmachine.org/2011/09/20/lets-build-a-compiler/

over the last 30 years. Some of these are published, others are not. This book reflects my experiences in undertaking these projects.

Let's first state what an interpreter is. An **interpreter** reads a program and translates it into an intermediate form which is then immediately executed. A **compiler**, on the other hand, reads a program and translates it into machine instructions which are executed at a later time. Interpreters will often work in an interactive mode where the state of a previous run is maintained. This is something that compilers most definitely do not do.

Given the size of the effort, I'm splitting the work into two or three smaller books. Part 1 (this book), covers lexical analysis along with an introduction to syntax analysis. The second book, Part 2, will cover more syntax analysis and code generation. I've chosen to publish the books in parts so that I can get the material out faster.

In this series of books, I will describe a language I developed some time ago, called Rhodus, named after my pet dog. The full version of the Rhodus language is procedural and has elements of Python, Basic and Pascal. The language has support for modules, exception handling, labeled matrices, complex numbers, and a reasonably well featured interactive command line interface that supports history and command completion. The book series is going to cover the development of this language using Object Pascal.

In this book, as with Ball, we won't be using a compiler generator such as Yacc or ANTLR, but will write all the code from scratch without any assistance from external applications.

1.2   Why Object Pascal?

I suppose the biggest question a reader might ask is why I picked Object Pascal.[4] Surely it would have been better to have used Java, C#, C, or even Python as the language to write an interpreter? Perhaps, but there are already books that describe compilers written in these languages, especially C, and there are numerous projects online that use these same programming languages to either write compilers, or less frequently, interpreters. In the Java and C#, world, we have the open source Jython and Iron Python as excellent examples of interpreters written in Java and C# respectively. There is also a multitude of compilers and some interpreters to be found on sites such as SourceForge and GitHub, which are worth reviewing. Of course, in most of these cases, all you have is the raw code without any explanatory text, and many of them remain unfinished. Examples of open source interpreters I've come across include Euler, Algae, Boo, fudgit, jbasic, nasal, RLab, yjasl, yorick, and the list goes on. Most of these are written in C (that's right, not C++).

In contrast, there are relatively few examples of compilers and interpreters written in Object Pascal. There is, of course, Free Pascal which is a compiler written in Object Pascal but there are very few interpreters. DWScript is an interpreter, but it isn't geared to be used in interactive mode by a human user. Likewise, RemObjects Pascal Script (https://

---

[4]This includes Free Pascal as well as the Object Pascal supplied with Embarcadero Delphi.

`www.remobjects.com/ps.aspx`) is also an interpreter written in Object Pascal, but again it's not meant for interactive use. There are also compilers of Delphi source code, such as Bieniek's PasParse (`https://github.com/Turbo87/PasParse`) and Yankovsky's well-known Delphi AST (`https://github.com/RomanYankovsky/DelphiAST`). I'm sure there are others. However, whereas there are a plethora of small interactive languages, especially various dialects of Basic, written in the likes of Java, C, Python, and C#, I was not able to find anything comparable that used Object Pascal. This suggests an opportunity to describe an interpreter written in Object Pascal.

Another reason for choosing Object Pascal is that it is such a nice language to program in. It's clean, meaning that there is a minimum of distracting punctuation that we see in languages such as C++. The only comparable language is C#, though the most recent versions of C# seem to be losing their simplicity as developers add on every kitchen sink they can find. For beginners, Object Pascal is easy to read, even to the uninitiated. It uses a fairly literal language which can put off those more used to a terser format. Many will complain about the need to spell out the keywords `begin` and `end`, but to a newcomer, they are relatively self-explanatory. `For` loops are likewise more literal than similar constructs found in other languages. However, like any language, it's also possible to write unintelligible code in Object Pascal.

Object Pascal has many things going for it. It's modern, and it had many concepts early on in its development that we now take for granted in more recently developed languages. These include exception and finally handling, properties, a full object model, reflection, interfaces, and so on. In the last ten years, Object Pascal has also acquired attributes, generics, operator overloading, etc. In addition, it can be programmed on a number of levels including assembler, procedural and object orientated. Finally, coupling Object Pascal with the VCL (Visual Component Library) or FMX (FireMonkey) brings the developer one of the easiest ways to create rich graphical user interfaces across all three major platforms.

Although we'll be using Object Pascal, it shouldn't be difficult to translate the code into other equally modern languages.

1.3   Target Audience

The target audience for this book is the novice, hobbyist, the new student, and the mid-level developer. As a result, I've kept the code as simple as possible, and I've avoided some of the more advanced features found in Object Pascal. Seasoned developers will likely be horrified that I won't be using any interfaces. The entire code is based on classes. Interfaces, of course, can be very useful, especially for decoupling an implementation from its public API. However, for the purposes of pedagogy, I want to keep things as straightforward as possible.

1.4 What is an Interpreter?

We briefly answered this question earlier, but I need to add more flesh to that description. I assume we are all familiar with a standard compiler. A compiler is a program that translates source code into machine code. The Delphi Object Pascal translator is a standard compiler. I searched for a good definition of an interpreter but found most of the definitions unsatisfying. The problem is, what criterion to use? Is it the internal workings of the interpreter that matter, or is it more related to what the user experiences?

Internally there are more similarities than differences between an interpreter and a compiler. For a start, they are both language translators. They take source code such as a = 2 and convert it into another language that can be executed. One of the differences often touted is the kind of language that results from the translation. Compilers generate raw machine code, a language that is as close to the hardware as possible. Being so close to the hardware means that execution tends to be very fast. The downside is that it's easy to make the program crash. In earlier times such crashes could bring the entire computer down.

Interpreters don't, in general, generate machine code but create code for a software layer that emulates hardware. The idea is that we can protect the worst effects of poor programming by insulating the programmer from the raw hardware. There are a number of languages that use an emulation layer; the most famous of these being Java and C#. However, the idea of using an emulation layer dates from the mid-1960s and 1970s. For example, both Smalltalk[5] and Pascal-P[6] used an emulation layer. In Java, the emulation layer is called the Java virtual machine. Traditionally the translation of source code into code that is run by an emulation layer has been the defining property of an interpreter. However, with the advent of scripting languages such as Python, R, Matlab, etc., things have become less clear-cut. The picture is even more complicated because the Java compiler is also a hybrid, generating at runtime both compiled and virtual machine instructions. We also have Julia[7], which behaves like an interpreter, but internally compiles code much closer to the hardware by using LLVM.

For our purpose, we will define an interpreter in terms of the user experience rather than translation technology. I suspect most of us have used scripting languages such as Python, R, etc. These languages are popular for a number of reasons, but one of them is because operationally they are not like Java or C#. When we run a Java or C# program, we start it, it runs, then finishes. What makes scripting languages so different is that between runs, the state of the program is still active. This allows us to do interactive programming. Rather than compile, run and stop, we can have an iterative loop of loop (compile, run). This is sometimes referred to as REPL, or "run, eval, print, loop".

This will, I am sure, ruffle the odd feather, but for this book, I will define an interpreter as something that maintains state between compilations. Users interact directly with the com-

---

[5]https://en.wikipedia.org/wiki/Smalltalk
[6]https://en.wikipedia.org/wiki/P-code_machine
[7]https://julialang.org/

piler and the runtime system via an interactive shell. Figure 1.1 illustrates the differences.

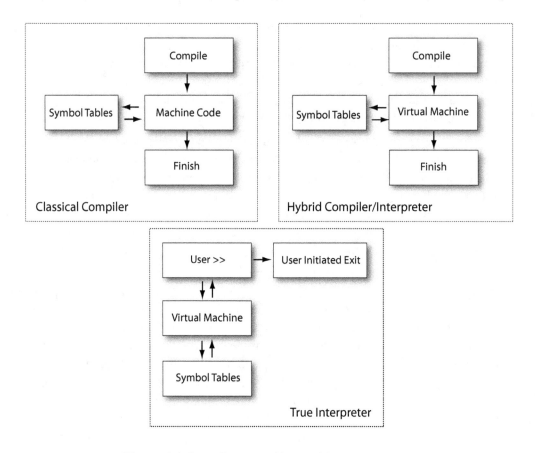

Figure 1.1 Compilers, Hybrids and Interpreters.

1.5 Parts of an Interpreter

Over the years, a standard information and processing pipeline has been developed when designing an interpreter or compiler. The pipeline follows a strict order, starting with lexical scanning, syntax parsing, semantic analysis, code generation, and finally execution (Figure 1.2).

1.5.1 Lexical analysis

The first phase is the scanner or lexical analysis stage. The purpose of this stage is to break the source code into tokens to make life easier for the following stages. Some terminology is frequently used in lexical analysis which merits review. The first is the *lexeme*. A lexeme is a single identifiable sequence of one or more characters. For example, these can include keywords such as end, while etc, identifiers such as myVariable, count, etc, literal values such as numbers and strings, and punctuation characters such as '(', '+' etc.

Lexical analysis identifies the lexemes and converts them to *tokens*. Tokens are often simple integers that represent the lexemes. For example, a keyword such as while might be represented by the number 5, or the symbol '+' might be represented by the number 12. Each lexeme will have a token value. In addition, some tokens will have additional information. For example, a token representing a number will also have associated with it the actual number.

1.5.2 Syntax analysis

Syntax analysis, also known as parsing, takes the stream of tokens generated by lexical analysis and makes sure that the order of tokens correctly matches the grammar of the language. For example, the expression $a + b$ is grammatically correct, whereas $+ab$ is grammatically incorrect.

The second function of syntax analysis is to arrange the tokens into a more convenient form that reflects the syntax of the source code. This is often called the intermediate code and is achieved by creating an *abstract syntax tree* or AST. The reason why is it called abstract is that some of the tokens such as parentheses have been removed from the description and any structure that was defined by the parentheses is now implicitly encoded in the AST structure.

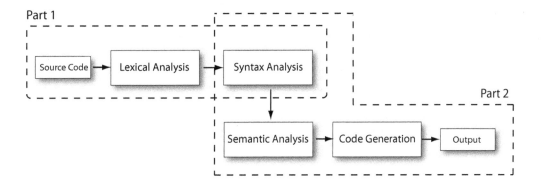

Figure 1.2 Stages involved in processing source code.

1.5.3 Semantic analysis

Once the syntax analysis has created an AST, it is possible to more fully analyze the original source code. The purpose of the semantic analysis phase is to make sure that the statements made in the source code actually make sense. For example, the following English sentence is grammatically correct but makes no sense: "The green apple ate a juicy house". For dynamically typed languages such as Python (i.e., where we don't declare variables to have specific types), there isn't much semantic analysis to do. For a strongly typed language such as Object Pascal, however, type checking is very important, and analysis will occur during the semantic analysis phase.

1.5.4   Code Generation

The final stage is to convert the AST into executable code. For an interpreter, this will often be in the form of bytecode although there are instances where the execution is done directly from the AST. Sometimes, depending on the sophistication of the interpreter, there can also be an optimization stage just before the code is generated. This is where inefficient code is removed or modified. For example, in the expression 0*(a1 + a2 + a3) there is little point in carrying out the sum, a1+a+2+a3 because of the multiplication by zero. An optimization stage would reduce this expression to a simple zero. In addition, if this were assigned to a variable b, and b was found to be used nowhere else, the entire assignment could be removed without affecting the program's function.

1.5.5   REPL (Interactive Console)

REPL stands for read–eval–print loop. In my mind, a REPL is what distinguishes a compiler from an interpreter. Those who were brought up on Basic or Lisp will be very familiar with the idea: Type code at a prompt and immediately get feedback. The rapid feedback from a REPL makes it an ideal environment to explore new ideas. Reading some comments online you'd think that interactive programming was only recently invented, but of course, it's been with us much longer. What differs today is the sophistication. At its very basic level, a REPL will allow a user to type text at a prompt, hit return, and the code will be executed. If the code generates output, then it is displayed to the user, and the interpreter is ready again to accept input.

A more sophisticated REPL will have a variety of features to enhance productivity. The most common of these are:

1. History of previously executed code

2. Auto-completion of variables, objects, libraries, language keywords, etc.

3. Ability to enter multiple lines of code

4. Additional commands to access the host file system

5. Graphical support for plotting etc.

6. Listing methods available within an object or library

7. An interactive help system to get more information on methods etc.

In this series of books, we will slowly enhance a Rhodus REPL to support some of these features.

Further Reading

1. Peter John Brown (1979) Writing Interactive Compilers and Interpreters, Wiley. **A classic for those interested in writing interpreters.**

2. Payne and Payne (1982) Implementing BASICSs: How BASICSs Work, Reston Publishing.

3. Brian W. Kernighan and Rob Pike (1984) The Unix Programming Environment, Prentice Hall. **The appendix describes the staged development of the HOC calculator. Very readable and it will teach you a lot.**

4. Brinch Hansen (1985) Brinch Hansen on Pascal Compilers, Prentice Hall. **Describes in detail the development of a Pascal compiler in Pascal. Good theory introduction.**

5. Alfred V. Aho, Ravi Sethi, Jeffrey D. Ullman (1986) Compilers Principles, Techniques and Tools, Addison-Wesley (The so-called Dragon book) **Get a copy once you understand more about compilers and interpreters, it's <u>not</u> a good book for beginners.**

6. Jack Crenshaw (1988-1995) Let's Build a Compiler, online at `https://compilers.iecc.com/crenshaw/`. **An online resource on how to write a compiler using Pascal, liked by many.**

7. Peter Pechenberg and Hanspeter Mossenbock (1989) A Compiler Generator for Microcomputers, Prentice Hall. **The theory and introductory chapters are short and clear.**

8. Jeremy P. Bennett (1990) Introduction to Compiling Techniques, McGraw-Hill. **Build a compiler using Yacc, outputs a machine code like instruction set for an emulated machine. The text is straightforward and easy to read.**

9. Ronald Mak (1991) Writing Compilers & Interpreters, An Applied Approach, Wiley. **Build a Pascal compiler using C. If you know C I highly recommend this book. It covers a lot of ground. There is little discussion of theory, but that's ok.**

10. Henk Alblas and Albert Nymeyer (1996) Practice and Principles of Compiler Building in C, Prentice Hall.

11. Niklaus Wirth (1996) Compiler Construction.

12. Andrew W. Appel (1997) Modern Compiler Implementation in C, Cambridge. **Liked by many; it's a book that can grow on you. There is also a Java version.**

13. Allen I. Holub (2000) Compiler Design in C, Prentice Hall.

14. Grune et al. (2000) Modern Compiler Design (Now with a second edition 2012) **Readable theory with some practical discussion.**

15. Terence Parr (2010) Language Implementation Patterns, Pragmatic Bookshelf. **Uses a pattern-based approach. This isn't to everyone's taste perhaps but it's modern and discusses many techniques currently in use which you'll find difficult to locate elsewhere. Also talks a lot about ANTLR, not surprising since the author is the main ANTLR developer.**

16. Des Watson (2017) A Practical Approach to Computer Construction, Springer. **As the book says, it's practical, recommended for the beginner. Lots of text and less code, but the text is very readable.**

17. Thorsten Ball. Writing an Interpreter in GO (Date: 2017-2018) `https://interpreterbook.com/`. **A unique book that goes through the building of an interpreter. The inspiration for this book. The book is generally light on theory, but given its objectives, that's ok.**

18. Thorsten Ball. Writing a Compiler in GO (Date: June 2018) `https://interpreterbook.com/`. **Another unique offering from Ball, this time focusing on building the virtual machine.**

2

The Rhodus Language

2.1 The Rhodus Language: Version 1

Let's first describe version one of the language we'll use for the interpreter. We'll call the language Rhodus after my dog Rhody. As with most introductions to a new language, we'll start with Hello World:

```
println ("Hello World")
```

The method `println` writes its arguments to the console together with a newline.

2.2 File Extension

The file extension `.rh` will be used to indicate a Rhodus source file.

2.3 Commenting

There are two ways to add comments to a Rhodus program: Single line and block commenting. Single line commenting uses the '`//`' start code to begin a comment. A line comment ends at the line's new line character. For example, the following uses line commenting:

```
// Start the Program Here
println ("Type some data");

answer = 30+15;  // Don't forget to do the calculation
```

Type	Comment	Examples
Integers	32 bits with one bit reserved for the sign. An integer will cover the range: $-2,147,483,648\ldots2,147,483,647$	$3, -34$
Double	A floating point number of type double uses 8 bytes. Supports approximately 15 digits of precision in a range from: 2.23×10^{-308} to 1.79×10^{308}	1.23, 3.456E-3, 0.324, 1E4
Boolean	A single byte that represents True or False.	`True, False`
String	A sequence of unicode characters. Maximum length 2^{30} characters.	"A string"
Lists	A indexable but heterogenous list of data types, including lists.	`{5,6,7,{True, 3.14},...}`

Table 2.1 Data types in version one of Rhodus.

Sometimes it is desirable to comment out entire blocks of code or to add notes to a program. In such cases, it might be easier to use block commenting. A block comment starts with `'/*'` and ends with `'*/'`. For example:

```
// Start the program here
println ("Type some data");

/*
for i = 1 to 10 do
    println ("This will not be printed");
end
*/

// Don't forget to do the calculation
answer = 30*15;
```

2.4 Data Types

Rhodus version one will support a limited number of types that include: integer, double, string, Boolean and lists. Lists are heterogeneous collections of data, very much like the Python list. We will reserve square brackets for a future array/matrix type (to match Matlab) and therefore use curly brackets for lists. A summary of the data types is given in Table 2.1.

Version one won't support hexadecimal notation or the variety of integer types one finds in professional languages. These may be added to version two.

Strings are delimited by double quotes and can include escape characters. Only a few escape characters are supported, these include '\t' which represent tab, '\n' the new line and '\r' carriage return. '\\' is used to represent the backslash itself.

2.5   Variable Names

Following the tradition of other computer languages, variable names in Rhodus are case-sensitive. This means that the variable names Glucose and glucose are distinct. All variable names must start with either a letter or an underscore followed by any number of digits, letters or underscore characters. Thus the following variable names are legitimate: abcd, _abcd, abcd_6_efgh whereas the following are illegal: 23AB, abcd&efgh, $abcd.

Variables do not need to be declared but can be brought into play at any time and can be used to store any Rhodus data type.

```
a = 2.3
b = 4.567E-2
c = 4564
first_name = "John"
animals = { "dog", "cat", "mouse" }
```

Both string and lists will be mutable. This is in contrast to many other languages where strings are immutable. It will thus be possible to type:

```
a = "hello"
a[3] = 'L'
b = {1,2,3}
b[1] = 22
```

Indexing will be from zero for strings and lists.

2.6   Expressions and Operators

The full set of supported arithmetic and Boolean operations is shown in Table 2.2.

Examples:

```
2^3
10 div 3
10 mod 3
a + b
a + b*(6 - x)^3 + x/5
```

Operation	Symbol	Operation	Symbol
Addition	+	Logical and	and
Subtraction	-	Logical or	or
Multiplication	*	Logical not	not
Division	/	Logical xor	xor
Remainder	mod	Equality	==
Integer Division	div	Comparison	>, >=, <, <=, !=
Power	^		

Table 2.2 Arithmetic, Relational and Boolean Operators

```
6 == b
(a < b) and (c > 6)
```

In version one we won't support mathematical functions such as a sine, or log because these will be provided through a math module and we won't be supporting modules in version one, though I might change my mind on this last point.

The only support for lists in version one is creating lists using the following syntax:

```
aList = {1,2,3,4,5}
```

and indexing elements in a list:

```
println (aList[i])
a[2] = 3.14;
```

and printing whole lists:

```
println (aList)
```

Additional list functionality will be provided once modules are implemented by creating a built-in list module.

2.7 Semicolons

The semicolon is used to separate statements. This is very similar to how semicolons are dealt with in Pascal. This can create situations that are sometimes difficult for newcomers to understand. For example, the lack of a semicolon at the end of an `else` statement or the absence of a semicolon on the statement just before an `end`. We will come back to this topic later in the book.

```
a = 4;
a = 5; b = 7;
a = 2;
```

Newline characters such as line feed are not considered part of the syntax of the language except to mark the end of a one-line comment.

2.8 Output

Version one will only have limited support for output to the console. This will include the `print` and `println` statements. These take a comma-separated list of expressions. The `println` version will also issue a newline. In version one, reading is not supported because a later version will provide a specific console library as well as input and output to files. Once the console library is available, it is likely that the top-level `print` and `println` statements will be deprecated.

2.9 Control Statements

Rhodus supports the following control structures, `if`, `while`, `for` and `repeat`. They operate in a similar manner to equivalent control structures in other languages. Rhodus uses the keyword end to terminate a loop structure. We don't use curly brackets to delimit blocks as other languages do because these are reserved for lists.

2.9.1 While

The while loop will execute the enclosing statements as long as the expression is true. The chief characteristic of `while` loops is that the test is at the start of each iteration. While loops **must always** be terminated with the `end` keyword even if the `while` loop only has a single statement. Round brackets around the expression are not required. While loops can be nested. The break statement (see below) can be used to unconditionally exit the while loop.

```
while expression do
    statements
end;
```

Example:

```
a = 5
while a >= 0 do
    println ("Count down", a);
```

```
    a = a - 1
end;
```

2.9.2   Repeat/Until

repeat/until is another loop structure. Whereas in a while loop the test is applied at the
start, in a repeat/until loop the test is applied at the end. This means that statements within
the loop will be executed at least once. The break statement (see below) can be used to
unconditional exit from the repeat/until loop.

```
repeat
   statements
until expression;
```

Example:

```
a = 10;
repeat
  println ("Value of a = ", a);
  a = a - 1
until a < 2;
```

2.9.3   For loop

The for loop creates a loop that is dependent on a counter that is incremented or decre-
mented. The for loop must be terminated with an end keyword no matter how many statements there are within the body of the loop. The for loop terminates when the loop counter
passes the final value in the loop. The break statement can be used to unconditionally break
out of a for loop.

```
for name = expression to/downto expression do
      statements
end;
```

Example:

```
for i = 1 to 10 do
    println (i)
end;

for x = 5 to 20 do
    println (x)
end;

for x = 10 downto 1 do
    println ("Count down:", x)
```

```
   end;

   for x = lowValue to highValue do
       println ("Value = ", x)
   end;
```

2.9.4 Break

Each of the loop based control statements also supports the `break` keyword that allows unconditional escape from the loop.

For example:

```
   x = 1;
   repeat
     x = x + 1;
     if x > 5 then
         break
     end
   until x > 10;
```

```
   for i = 1 to 10 do
       if i == 5 then
           break
       end;
       println (i);
   end;
```

2.9.5 Conditionals

The conditional statement `if` is fairly standard. It comes in two versions:

`if...then` and `if...then...else`

For the first version, if the expression is `True` then the body of the conditional is executed which must be terminated with the end keyword. The expression must resolve to a Boolean value. Expressions that resolve to an integer, floating point or other data type are undefined and will generate a runtime error.

```
   if expression then
       statements
   end;
```

The second form of the `if` statement is one involving `else`. If the expression is `True` then the first set of statements are executed. If the expression is `False`, the statement within the `else` body of code is executed. The entire structure must be terminated with the end keyword. The problem of the 'dangling-else' statement is avoided (See Chapter 6 for further details) by use of the final end keyword. An example of a nested if/then/else statement is given below.

```
if expression then
    statements
else
    statements
end;
```

Example:

```
if (a < 9) or (b < 12) then
    println ("Condition met")
end;
```

```
if True then
    println ("It's True")
else
    println ("It's False")
end;
```

Nested if statements:

```
if a < 5 then
    println ("It's True");
    if b < 10 then
        println ("Inner if statement")
    end
else
    println ("It's False")
end;
```

```
if ... then
  statements
  if ... then
      statements
      if ... then
          statements
      else
          statements
      end
  else
      statements
  end
else
    println ("It's False")
```

```
end;
```

2.10   User-Defined Functions

Rhodus supports user-defined function much like other programming languages. Some example code will make this clear:

```
function add (a, b)
   return a + b
end;

// Recursive function
function fib (n)
   if n <= 1 then
      return n
   end;
   return fib (n-1) + fib (n-2)
end;
```

Arguments can be passed by value or by reference. Integers, doubles and Boolean values are passed by value but can be passed by reference by using the `ref` keyword, for example:

```
function sum (ref x, y)
   x = 5; // Changes x outside of sum
   y = 5; // y does not change outside of sum
end;
```

For larger structures such as lists or strings, these are passed automatically by reference. For example, passing a list to a function and changing a list inside the function will change it's value outside the function:

```
function sum (alist)
   sum = 0;
   for i = 1 to 10 do
      sum = sum + alist[i]
   end;
   return sum
end;
```

A function doesn't have to return anything to the caller, but if a function does return a value, this is done by calling `return` as shown in the examples above. Functions don't have to have arguments in which case a function call is made with the name followed by empty brackets, for example:

```
function sum
```

```
   return 2 + 3
end;

x = sum();
```

The full syntax for version 1 of the language will be given in Chapter 6 .

2.11   Memory Management

Strings and lists are stored on the heap. This means there are memory management issues with these data types. In version one, memory management will be simple. Later on we can consider more sophisticated memory management such as reference counting or mark and sweep techniques. Consider the following two assignments:

```
a = "A string"
a = "Another string"
```

The second assignment will free the memory allocated for a and then assign the new string to a. The same applies to lists.

2.11.1   Copy Assignments

In version one an assignment will result in a copy made of the right-side and assigned to the left-side. For example:

```
a = "A string"
b = a
```

The second assignment will cause a copy of the contents of a to be made and assigned to the variable b.

2.12   Example Programs Using Version 1

The following shows some example Rhodus programs.

```
principal = 500;
rate = 0.04;
numYears = 10;
year = 1;
while year <= numYears do
   principal = principal + principal*rate;
   println ("Year: ", year, " Bank Balance: ", principal);
   year = year + 1
```

```
end
```

```
// Is the number odd or even?
value = 7;
if value mod 2 == 0 then
    println ("The number is even")
else
    println ("The number is odd")
end
```

```
// Check if the number provided by the user is an Armstrong
// number or not.
sum = 0;

// find the sum of the cube of each digit
temp = num;
while temp > 0 do
    digit = temp div 10;
    sum = sum + digit^3;
    temp = temp / 10
end;

// display the result
if num == sum then
    println(num,"is an Armstrong number")
else
    println(num,"is not an Armstrong number")
end
```

```
x = 55;
repeat
  println (x);
  x = x - 1
until x < 20;
```

For Loop Example:

```
// Check if n is a prime
function IsPrime (n)
  if n == 1 then
    return False;
  end;
  for m = 2 to (n div 2) do
    if n mod m == 0 then
      return False
    end
  end;
```

```
   return True;
end;

println (IsPrime (10))
```

```
// Recursive version for computing the Fibonacci Sequence
// Fn = Fn-1 + Fn-2, where Fo = 0 and F1 = 0
function fib (x)
   if ((x == 0) or (x == 1)) then
      return x
   end;
   return fib (x-1) + fib (x-2)
end;

f = fib (10000);
println (f);
```

```
// The list is always passed as a reference. This allows us to modify
// the list inside the function. There is no support for retrieving the
// length of a list yet, so we pass the length manually.
function bubbleSort (a, length)
   for i = 0 to length - 1 do
      for j = i+1 to length - 1 do
         if (a[i] > a[j])
            temp = a[i];
            a[i] = a[j];
            a[j] = temp;
         end
      end
   end
end;

// Sort the following array
alist = {5,2,6,7,3,2,5,1,4,9};
lengthOfList = 9;
bubbleSort (alist, lengthOfList);
println (alist);
```

2.13   Version 1.5 and 2 Highlights

In version 1.5, modules will be added so that code stored in a file gets a namespace. For example, the following describes a hypothetical math module:

```
module math

function add (a, b)
```

```
    return a + b
end;

function sub (a, b)
    return a - b
end;

end
```

It will be possible to import modules using the `import` keyword, for example:

```
import math

println (math.add (4,5))
```

With module support in version 1.5, we will be able to support the following built-in modules: I/O, math, strings, and lists.

Version 2 will continue to develop Rhodus and include the following additional features:

1. Labeled arrays

2. Complex Numbers

3. Code types

4. Exception handling

5. Module for array manipulation

6. Records

3

Lexical Analysis

3.1 Introduction

We begin by first writing the lexical analyser, also called the scanner. The purpose of the lexical analyser is to break the source code into a series of tokens to make life easier for the following stages. We will define a number of terms commonly used in the literature. These include:

1. Lexeme: a single identifiable sequence of one or more characters. For example, keywords such as `'end'`, `'while'` etc, identifiers such as `'myVariable'`, `'count'`, literal values such as numbers and strings or punctuation characters such as `'('`, `'+'` etc.

2. Token: whereas a lexeme is a sequence of characters that identifies a lexical unit, a token is often a simple integer representation of the lexeme. Tokens are often a pair of values that includes the integer representing the type of lexeme found and an attribute that includes any additional information about the token.

The lexical analyser receives a steady stream of characters from the source code and translates the characters into a series of tokens. In code we will represent tokens as simple integers using an enumerated type together with any additional information that is pertinent to the token. Such information would include the values for literal numbers or strings, and the string representation of variables.

The lexical analyzer also has the important function to remove comment statements and extraneous white space. This allows the subsequent syntax analysis stage be more focused

	Token	Value		Token	Value
1	tIdentifier	'a'	11	tIdentifier	'a'
2	tEquals	'='	12	tEquals	'='
3	tInteger	2	13	tIdentifier	'a'
4	tSemiColon	';'	14	tMinus	'-'
5	tRepeat	'repeat'	15	tInteger	1
6	tPrintln	'println'	16	tSemiColon	';'
7	tLeftParenthesis	'('	17	tUntil	'until'
8	tIdentifier	'a'	18	tIdentifer	'a'
9	tRightParenthesis	')'	19	tEquals	'='
10	tSemiColon	';'	20	tInteger	1

Table 3.1 Tokens generated from an input program.

on its core function, which is to analyze syntax. The lexical analyzer can also identify some error conditions. For example, if the input text has illegal characters, strings that have unterminated quotation marks, unterminated comments or numbers in the input text that are not within the numeric bounds. Figure 3.1 show the flow of information between the lexical analysis and the syntax analysis stage. The lexical analyser will implement a key method, called nextToken that is used by the syntax analyser to retrieve tokens.

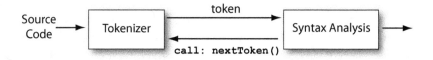

Figure 3.1 Overall plan for the lexical analyzer.

Given an input string such as:

```
a = 2;
repeat
   println (a);
   a = a - 1;
until a = 0
```

The lexical analyzer will convert the string into the list of tokens found in Table 3.1.

Figure 3.2 shows the overall design for the lexical analyzer. It starts at the top with the input of source code. Then through a series of stages, it eventually generates tokens.

The formal way to describe a lexical analyzer is to use state diagrams which describe changes in state as a result of an event. The events, in this case, are the detection of letters, numbers, etc. which indicate the type of token we are likely to retrieve. In some cases the use of state transition diagrams is overkill, and in my mind, they can make the code more difficult to understand (you'd need the state diagram in front of you). Lexical analyzers for our purpose are sufficiently straightforward that they can be written without having to reference a state diagram. Hence we won't be using them here.

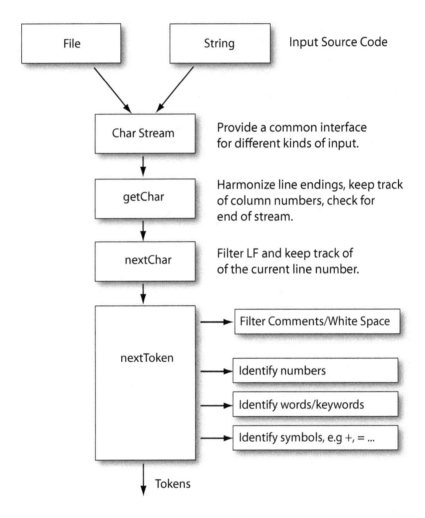

Figure 3.2 Overall design for the lexical analyzer.

We will be writing our lexical analyser by hand and we won't be using automated systems such as *lex* which allow a programmer to specify the lexemes and tokens and the program will automatically generate a lexical analyser. Those systems, though tempting to use, tend to be less flexible.

3.1.1 Availability of source code

If you want to build the lexical analyzer as we go along, you'll need to create a Delphi group. There will ultimately be a number of projects within the group, including three console applications (simple tester, unit tester, and the start of a REPL). In addition, for those who'd like a GUI, there is also a simple GUI application that will display the list of tokens in a given a string or file. The project group will be described in more detail in Chapter 4.

You have access to all the code on Github at:

`https://github.com/penavon/BookPart1`.

The code for this chapter and the next two can be found in the folder:

`LexicalAnalysis_Chap3_4_5`

Remember, when you ever need to load code from the GitHub repository, always load the group file, in this case `RhodusLexicalGroup.groupproj`.

3.2 The initial API

Let's begin by defining a minimal API for the lexical analyzer.

The lexical analyzer is usually the easiest part to write, and its interface can be equally simple. In fact, at minimum, it only needs to support two operations:

1. Load the source code into the lexical analyzer.

2. Retrieve the next token from the input stream.

Given this minimal requirement, let's define an API for our lexical analyzer:

```
procedure scanString (const str : string);
procedure nextToken;
```

Let's wrap these methods into a class we'll call `TScanner`:

```
TScanner = class (TObject)
    private
    public
       procedure scanString (const str : string);
       procedure nextToken;
end;
```

The parser will use `nextToken` to fetch the next token in the input stream. We might use this class in the following way:

```
sc := TScanner.Create;
sc.scanString (mySourceCode);
```

```
sc.nextToken;
while sc.token <> tEndOfStream do
    begin
    ...do stuff with the token
    sc.nextToken;
    end;
```

A couple of new ideas have been introduced in the above code. The first is that the lexical analyzer has a constructor TScanner.Create. The second is that the TScanner class has a public read-only property called token of type TTokenCode. This type can be quite simple, in fact, we'll use a simple enumeration. At the moment it has a single entry, tEndOfStream. Finally, I've introduced our first token which is called tEndOfStream. tEndOfStream will be used to mark the end of the input text so that we'll know when to stop. Let's expand our type and class definition to be:

```
TTokenCode = (tEndOfStream);
TScanner = class (TObject)
    private
    public
        constructor Create;
        procedure scanString (const str : string);
        procedure nextToken;
        property  token : TTokenCode read [NOT YET DEFINED];
end;
```

At the moment we've not specified what the property token reads. We'll do that shortly, and so I've left the entry undefined.

3.2.1 Input streams

The next part to consider is how to implement the input stream. At the moment we have one input stream coming from a string that is handled by scanString. We might also want to get the source code from a file. To service this, we'll need to add a new method which we'll call scanFile (fileName).

The question then is what is behind scanString and scanFile? We can take a number of different approaches here. We could open a file using the traditional assignFile and reset pair of calls and use the file method read to retrieve the characters one at a time. This works for a file, but we'd have to write something different to handle a string.

Another approach is to load the file into a string and have an ungainly set of counters and pointers showing us where we are in the string as we read the characters one by one. This approach seems to be fairly common. Since we're using Delphi or Free Pascal, a far better solution is use a TStreamReader and a TStream. Streams provide a common interface for reading and writing data to different media such as memory, strings and of course files. They offer a lot more flexibility, and we can use the same code to access a file or a string.

They also have the advantage that they are easy to use.

TStreamReader is a class that can work with a number of different types of streams, including strings and files. When a TStreamReader is constructed it takes as an argument an actual stream of type TStream. TStream types can be string streams or file streams. These are called TStringStream and TFileStream respectively. You might wonder why not use these directly instead of going via TStreamReader? TStreamReader has a number of advantages. First TStreamReader has a property called EndOfStream which I think we'll find useful. Secondly, it has a Peek method that allows us to lookahead one character without consuming the character. We might find that useful in the future too. With these in mind we can write the two methods, scanString and scanFile as follows:

```
procedure TScanner.scanString (const str : string);
begin
  FStreamReader := TStreamReader.Create(TStringStream.Create (str, TEncoding.UTF8));
  FStreamReader.OwnStream;
  startScanner;
end;

procedure TScanner.scanFile (const fileName : string);
begin
  FStreamReader := TStreamReader.Create(
          TBufferedFileStream.Create (filename, fmOpenRead), TEncoding.UTF8);
  FStreamReader.OwnStream;
  startScanner;
end;
```

In scanFile, we will use TBufferedFileStream instead of TFileStream. TBuffered-FileStream has much better performance; otherwise, it has the same functionality. We need to declare a new variable, FStreamReader in the TScanner class that will be a reference to our stream object. The TEncoding.UTF8 in the stream argument is an encoding of text files that is backward compatible with ASCII encoded files and Unicode encoded files. This means we'll be able to read both Unicode and traditional ASCII text.

There is one little complication we need to be aware of, who owns the stream? When we create a TStreamReader we pass to it a TStream object. By default however TStream-Reader will not take responsibly for freeing the TStream instance when it is itself freed. This means if we free the FStreamReader variable, the TStream handle will not be freed. If a file handle is associated with the stream, it won't be closed either. This is bad because the next time we or anyone else try to open the same file again, we'll get an error indicating that it is already open. To avoid this and to make things simpler we can specify that the TStreamReader owns the stream. We do this with the statement: FStream-Reader.OwnStream. Now, when we free FStreamReader we'll free the reader as well as the associated stream.

The last thing we do in the scan methods is call a method called startScanner. This will initialize some variables and retrieve the first character from the stream. We'll come back

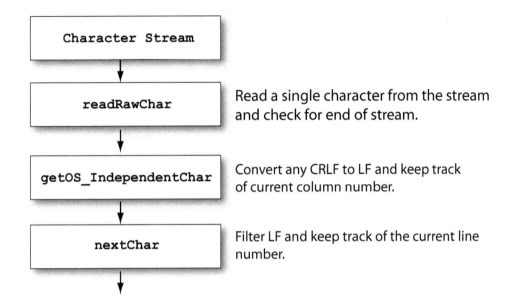

Figure 3.3 Flow diagram for retrieving characters from the input stream.

to this later.

Let's update the class definition to accommodate these changes:

```
TTokenCode = (tEndOfStream);
TScanner = class (TObject)
    private
        FStreamReader  : TStreamReader;
        procedure    startScanner;
    public
        constructor Create;
        procedure    scanString (const str : string);
        procedure    scanFile (const str : string);
        procedure    nextToken;
        property     token : TTokenCode read [NOT YET DEFINED];
end;
```

3.2.2 Retrieving characters

At this point, we still can't run any code. A couple of things remain, the most important is to flesh out nextToken. Before we can write nextToken we need to create some helper routines, this includes readRawChar, getOS_IndependentChar and nextChar. The relationship between the three methods and a summary of what they do is given in Figure 3.3.

The first of these routines readRawChar reads a single character directly from the stream.

When we reach the end of the stream the `TStreamReader` property called `EndOfStream` is set true. When this point is reached, we'll return the ASCII character 255 or $FF hex. We'll call this character `EOF_CHAR`, and we'll define it as a constant at the top of the lexical analyzer.

We will also introduce two new private variables `FColumnNumber`, that will track the column we're at on a particular line and `FLineNumber` that will track the current line we're on. These variables will be updated in the next few methods.

`readRawChar` is shown below. It first checks whether we're at the end of the stream. If we are it frees the stream and returns the end of stream character `EOF_CHAR`. If we're not at the end of the stream, it goes ahead and returns the next character by calling the stream read method. One thing to remember is that the read method returns an integer and we must cast it to a char to obtain our character. It also increments the `FColumnNumber` indicating that we've moved one column along the current line.

```
1   // Get a single char from the input stream
2   function TScanner.readRawChar : Char;
3   begin
4     if FStreamReader = nil then
5        exit (char (EOF_CHAR));
6
7     if FStreamReader.EndOfStream  then
8        begin
9        freeAndNil (FStreamReader);
10       result := char (EOF_CHAR);
11       end
12    else
13       begin
14       inc (FColumnNumber);
15       result := Char (FStreamReader.Read);
16       end
17  end;
```

I added a safety feature to the start of `readRawChar` to stop anyone from calling the method with a closed stream though it is very unlikely that this will happen.

There is a slight complication if we want our scanner to work on Windows as well as on a Mac OS or Linux based computer. The problem is that different operating systems treat the end of a line in a text file differently. On Unix based operating systems such as the variant found on the Mac OS, a line ending is indicated by a single line feed character, LF (ASCII value 10 or hex $0A). On windows a line ending is indicated by two characters, a carriage return (CR, ASCII 13 or hex $0D) followed by a line feed, that is CRLF. It would be nice to avoid this complication as soon as possible as it will save us a lot of distractions later on. For this reason, let's filter out this difference right after we read in a character. For readability, I thought it best to partition this off into a separate method called `getOS_IndependentChar`. This method will always return a single LF whether we're reading a file on Windows or a Unix/Linux like operating system.

getOS_IndependentChar first makes a call to readRawChar then checks if the retrieved character is an LF or CR, if it's neither it just returns the character.

```
function TScanner.getOS_IndependentChar : Char;
begin
  Fch:= readRawChar;
  if (Fch = CR) or (Fch = LF) then
     begin
     if Fch = CR then
        begin
        Fch := readRawChar;
        if Fch = LF then
           result := Fch
        else
           raise EScannerError.Create ('expecting line feed character');
        end
     else
        result := FCh;
     end
  else
     result := FCh;
end;
```

If it finds a CR or LF, it checks to see if it is a CR, if not then it must be an LF and it returns LF. If it is a CR, it retrieves another character using readRawChar, checks if it's an LF. If it is, it returns LF; otherwise, it issues an error. It will be illegal to use a text file (or string) that uses only a CR as a line ending. This is also the first time we've seen an exception raised. For exception handling, we define our own exception class EScannerException. This doesn't do anything special as yet but we might do something with it later on, so it's best to be prepared. EScannerError has the simple definition:

EScannerError = class (Exception)

With getOS_IndependentChar written we have one other method to write which we'll call nextChar. The purpose of this call is to replace any LF characters from getOS_IndependentChar with a space character, to reset the column number, FColumnNumber, to zero and increment the line number, FLineNumber, by one. The column number and line number will be used to keep track of where we are in the input stream and will be used when issuing error reports to the user.

You may be wondering why not combine nextChar with getOS_IndependentChar and avoid a second layer? The reason for the two calls is to make it easier to deal with comments that end with a new line. For example, the comment starting with '//' is terminated at a new line and in this instance we want an unfiltered method to retrieve the character. When we deal with comments, this will hopefully become clearer.

```
// Return the next character in the input stream.
// Filter out LF and increment the line number.
function TScanner.nextChar : Char;
```

```
begin
  result := getOS_IndependentChar;
  // Ignore LF and return the next character
  if result = LF do
     begin
     inc (FLineNumber);
     FColumnNumber := 0;
     result := ' ';
     end;
end
```

At this point we can return to the method `startScanner` which was introduced when we described `scanString` and `scanFile`. `startScanner` is shown below:

```
procedure TScanner.startScanner;
begin
  FLineNumber := 1;
  FColumnNumber := 0;
  Fch := nextChar;
end;
```

This method does two important things, it initializes `FLineNumber` and `FColumnNumber` to their starting values and most importantly to retrieves the first character from the stream using `nextChar`. The character is stored in a private variable in the class called `Fch`. `Fch` is used to store the current character from the stream and is used by a number of higher level methods including for example `nextToken`. Whenever `nextChar` is used, it will update `Fch`.

The `TScanner` class now expands to the following:

```
TTokenCode = (tEndOfStream);
TScanner = class (TObject)
    private
        Fch : Char;
        FColumeNumber, FLineNumber : integer;
        FStreamReader : TStreamReader;
        procedure  startScanner;
        function   readRawChar : Char;
        function   getOS_IndependentChar : Char;
        function   nextChar : Char;
    public
      constructor Create;
      procedure   scanString (const str : string);
      procedure   scanFile (const str : string);
      procedure   nextToken;
      property    token : TTokenCode read [NOT YET DEFINED];
end;
```

With `nextChar` written we can now work on `nextToken`.

3.2.3 Retrieving tokens: `nextToken`

`nextToken` is responsible for fetching the next token from the input stream. It doesn't return anything but updates the token property with the next token it found. The code is shown below.

There are three parts to the method: 1) skipping text that isn't important, such as whitespace and comments, 2) updating the line and column number in the token record so that we know which line we were on and at what column, and finally, 3) a series of `if` statements that are used to identify words, numbers, strings, end of stream and a catch-all `getSpecial`.

This method introduces a couple of new things. We've not seen the variable type `TToken-Record` before. This is a record that will store various kinds of information about the most recently scanned token. For example, if a number was scanned, then `FTokenRecord` will include the value of the number. In addition to these kinds of attributes, `FTokenRecord` can also store the line and column number for the token that is about to be scanned. We store this information with the token to ensure that when an error is detected either in the scanner or a future parser, the error message supplies the correct line and column number. We can't rely on the class variables `FLineNumber` and `FColumnNumber` because by the time we get the error these have been updated to just beyond the token and possibly to the next line if it's the last token in the line. Hence we must preempt the possibility of an error by storing these variables before we try to identify the token. We could probably dispense with the line and column variables in the class itself. This may offer an opportunity to do some refactoring later on.

```
1  procedure TScanner.nextToken;
2  begin
3    skipBlanksAndComments;
4
5    // Record the position of the token that we are about to identify
6    FTokenRecord.lineNumber := FLineNumber;
7    FTokenRecord.columnNumber := FColumnNumber;
8
9    if isLetter (Fch) then begin getWord;      exit; end;
10   if isDigit (FCh)  then begin getNumber;    exit; end;
11   if Fch = '"'      then begin getString;    exit; end;
12   if Fch = EOF_CHAR then
13      begin
14      FTokenRecord.Ftoken := tEndofStream;
15      if InMultiLineComment then
16         raise EScannerError.Create('detected unterminated comment,expecting "*/"');
17      exit;
18      end;
19
20   getSpecial;
21 end;
```

Let's next look at `skipBanksAndComments` which is the first thing we call in `nextToken`.

The code for this method is shown below. The method is more complicated than one might expect. In a previous version of the code I created tokens for the comment markers '//', '/*', and '*/' which simplified the logic but may not have been the conventional way to deal with comments. Instead, I opted to filter out comments and whitespace as we enter nextToken. skipBlanksAndComments calls two additional methods, skipSingleLine- Comment and skipMultiLineComment which we will come to shortly. Their names may betray their function.

```
1   procedure TScanner.skipBlanksAndComments;
2   begin
3     while Fch in [' ', TAB, '/']  do
4         begin
5         if Fch in [' ', TAB]  then
6             Fch := nextChar
7         else
8             begin
9             // Check for start of comment
10            if (char(FStreamReader.Peek) = '/') or (char(FStreamReader.Peek) = '*')then
11                begin
12                Fch := getOS_IndependentChar;
13                if Fch = '/' then // This kind of comment  // abc - single line
14                    skipSingleLineComment
15                else if Fch = '*' then // This kind of comment: /* abc */ - multiline
16                    skipMultiLineComment;
17                end
18            else
19                break;
20            end;
21        end;
22  end;
```

skipBlanksAndComments starts by checking for a space, a TAB or a '/' character. We want to filter out space or TAB characters. If the character is a '/' it could be the start of a comment. We'll continue looping in the while loop until the character is not one of these three at which point we get out. If Fch is one of the characters we're looking for, we proceed to the next section of code. The next statement (line 5) splits the flow depending on which character it was. If it was a space or a TAB we call nextChar and try again.

If the character was a '/' then we look to see if this is the start of a comment. If it's not, this is a valid character, and we return at the break statement on line 19. To figure out if we're at the start of a comment, we check if the next character is another '/' or a '*'. The first will start a single line comment and the '*' will start a multi-line comment. Note that we're using the Peek method available on the reader object FStreamReader. This is useful because if we aren't starting a comment, we don't want to have pulled the character out of the stream prematurely.

Assuming we are at the start of a comment we either call skipSingleLineComment or skipMultiLineComment. These two methods are fairly straightforward. In skipSingle-

LineComment the only thing we have to watch for is a potential end of stream. It's possible that a single line comment is the last line in the code and doesn't have a new-line in which case the terminating marker is an end of stream, i.e., EOF_CHAR. If the character is a LF, then the comment is naturally terminated. Note that if the comment was terminated with an end of stream marker, we don't want to make another call to nextChar. One final thing to note, we're using getOS_IndependentChar in the while loop because getOS_IndependentChar doesn't filter out the LF characters. However, it also doesn't increment the line number, so we have to add that right at the end of the skipSingleLineComment method.

```
procedure TScanner.skipSingleLineComment;
begin
  while (Fch <> LF) and (FCh <> EOF_CHAR) do
      Fch := getOS_IndependentChar;
  if FCh <> EOF_CHAR then
     Fch := nextChar
  inc (FLineNumber);
end;
```

The second method, skipMultiLineComment is shown below:

```
// Deal with this kind of comment  /* ..... */
procedure TScanner.skipMultiLineComment;
begin
  InMultiLineComment := True;
  // Move past '*'
  Fch := nextChar;
  while True do
     begin
     while (Fch <> '*') and (Fch <> EOF_CHAR) do
       Fch := nextChar;
     if Fch = EOF_CHAR then
       exit;

     FCh := nextChar;
     if FCh = '/' then
        begin
        Fch := nextChar;
        InMultiLineComment := False;
        break;
        end;
     end;
end;
```

The method first sets a new private variable in TScanner called InMultiLineComment to True. This will be used in nextToken to check whether we've reached the end of stream without closing the comment. We next skip over the expected '*' using nextChar before entering a while True loop. The while loop has two exits: The first exit happens if we ever retrieve an end of stream marker and the second is when we encounter the end of the comment. We also have to guard against a single '*' that might be in the comment text and not confuse a single '*' for the start of the end of the comment. If we detect the end of the comment we must remember to set InMultiLineComment to False. That completes the method. Note that we don't support nested multi-line comments.

We now return to nextToken. With the white space and comments filtered, nextToken starts to identify the current token by looking at the first character. All token information is stored in the record type TTokenRecord which has the following structure:

```
TTokenRecord = record
                 lineNumber, columnNumber : integer;
                 FToken        : TTokenCode;
                 FTokenString  : string;
                 FTokenFloat   : double;
                 FTokenInteger : integer;
               end;
```

Note that the property token pulls the current value of the token from this structure (FToken-Record). This means we can fill in the undefined method in the token property to be getTokenCode. We'll declare a new private variable FTokenRecord and the getTokenCode method which is shown below:

```
function TScanner.getTokenCode : TTokenCode;
begin
  result := FTokenRecord.FToken;
end;
```

The remainder of nextToken is to do with identifying specific tokens in the input stream. Of these, getNumber is the most complicated because it is used to identify integers, floats, and scientific notation. Let's begin with the simpler methods, getString and getWord.

It is worth noting first a stylistic issue before continuing. The series of if statements for detecting tokens could have been constructed using a series of nested if/else statements. It's a personal preference on my part not to use such nesting, but it is a perfectly reasonable thing to do. It would also be possible to use a switch statement as shown in the code below which may appeal to other developers:

```
1   // Alternative style for detecting tokens using a case statement
2   procedure TScanner.nextToken;
3   begin
4     skipBlanksAndComments;
5
6     // Record the position of the token that we are about to identify
7     FTokenRecord.lineNumber := FLineNumber;
8     FTokenRecord.columnNumber := FColumnNumber;
9
10    case Fch of
```

```
11        'a'..'z','A'..'Z','_' : getWord;
12        '0'..'9','.'          : getNumber;
13        '"'                   : getString;
14      EOF_CHAR :
15            begin
16            FTokenRecord.Ftoken := tEndofStream;
17            if InMultiLineComment then
18                raise EScannerError.Create ('detected unterminated
19                        comment, expecting "*/"');
20            exit;
21            end;
22        else
23            getSpecial;
24    end;
25  end;
```

Line 12 in the earlier nextToken method checks for EOF_CHAR. An EOF_CHAR character might be detected if we've been reading an unterminated comment. While reading a comment we set a flag, InMultiLineComment to True. When the comment is terminated, we set this flag back to False. We can, therefore, detect an unterminated comment by checking InMultiLineComment when we've reached the end of the stream. If it is set True then the comment was unterminated, and this is an error.

getString

getString is used to collect a string literal from the input stream.

At this point, we will introduce syntax diagrams, also called railroad diagrams. Such diagrams describe the grammatically correct structure for a particular 'sentence'. An alternative is to use the text-based Extended-Backus-Naur form (EBNF) which is frequently used for specifying programming languages. We'll consider grammars and EBNF in more detail in Chapter 6. Figure 3.4 shows a syntax diagram for a string. Hopefully, the diagrams are straightforward to understand, just follow the lines, starting on the left-hand side.

To read in a string, we start a loop that collects characters from the input stream until either the end of stream is reached, or we encounter a terminating double quotation character. Note that if we reach the end of the stream, it means we have an unterminated string which we will flag as an error. The code for getString is shown below.

```
begin
  FTokenRecord.FTokenString := '';
  FTokenRecord.FToken := tString;

  Fch := nextChar;
  while Fch <> EOF_CHAR do
      begin
      if Fch = '"' then
          begin
```

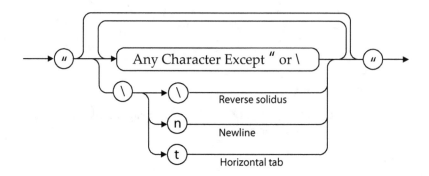

Figure 3.4 Syntax diagram for a literal string.

```
        Fch := nextChar;
        exit;
        end
    else
        begin
        FTokenRecord.FTokenString := FTokenRecord.FTokenString + Fch;
        Fch := nextChar;
        end
    end;
  raise EScannerError.Create ('string without terminating quotation mark');
end;
```

The first thing getString does is set up the token string value to empty and the token type to tString in the token record. After that we get the next character in the stream, start a while-loop and check if the character is a terminating quotation mark. Note that the string could be empty, namely "". If it is empty, we get the next character and exit. Otherwise, we add the most recently retrieved character to the growing FTokenString variable. This section is wrapped in a while-loop that checks for the end of stream. If the while-loop exits because it detected an end of stream we raise an exception indicating that the string has not been terminated correctly.

One thing we haven't done in the code is check for escape characters such as '\n'. This is easily done, however. Before we check for the end of the string quotation character, we see if the character is a '\'. If so, we check to see if it has one of the control letters after it. If it does we add the appropriate response to the growing token string. For example '\n' will result in sLineBreak added to the string. Note that two escape characters, '\\' indicate we add a single '\' to the string. Much like Python, we ignore any unrecognized escape characters and just pass them through. This code is shown below and completes the getString method:

```
if Fch = '\' then
    begin
```

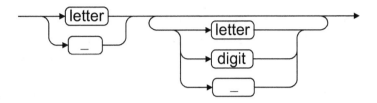

Figure 3.5 Syntax diagram for an identifier.

```
   Fch := nextChar;
   case Fch of
      '\' : FTokenRecord.FTokenString := FTokenRecord.FTokenString + '\';
      'n' : FTokenRecord.FTokenString := FTokenRecord.FTokenString + sLineBreak;
      'r' : FTokenRecord.FTokenString := FTokenRecord.FTokenString + CR;
      't' : FTokenRecord.FTokenString := FTokenRecord.FTokenString + TAB
      ;
   else
      FTokenRecord.FTokenString := FTokenRecord.FTokenString + '\' + Fch;
   end;
   Fch := nextChar;
end
```

getWord

The getWord method will be used to identify identifiers such as variable names and built-in keywords. For now, let's just focus on identifying variable names. The code for scanning in an identifier is actually quite straightforward. We define an identifier to be something that can start with a letter or an underscore and be followed by any number of letters, underscores, and digits. Figure 3.5 shows the syntax diagram for an identifier. The code for getWord is shown below and begins by setting the token string variable to empty.

```
// Scan in an identifier token
procedure TScanner.getWord;
begin
  FTokenRecord.FTokenString := '';

  while isLetter (Fch) or isDigit (Fch) do
     begin
     // Perhaps inefficient, but convenient
     FTokenRecord.FTokenString := FTokenRecord.FTokenString + Fch;
     Fch := nextchar;
     end;
  FTokenRecord.FToken := tIdentifier;
end;
```

We then start a loop to detect when we are no longer scanning a letter, underscore or digit. The `isLetter` method will test for letters and the underscore and is given below together with `isDigit`. The Delphi runtime library (RTL) does have built-in methods that mimic these functions, but I decided to provide my own because the built-in functions didn't see to behave as I expected. In the `getWord` code itself we accumulate the characters to form the word using a simple concatenation of strings. This is the same mechanism we used previously to accumulate a literal string. One could argue that a better way would be to use Delphi's built-in class `TStringBuilder` which is more efficient. For readability, concatenation is the easiest to show. Ideally, in the final application, time profiling could be done, and if string concatenation turns out to be a bottleneck, then the code could be optimized at that point. I tend to favor readability over performance until it becomes necessary to optimize due to inefficiencies. The last thing we do is set the token type to `tIdentifier`.

```
function TScanner.isLetter (ch : Char) : boolean;
begin
  result :=  ch in ['a'..'z', 'A'..'Z', '_'];
end;

function TScanner.isDigit (ch : Char) : boolean;
begin
  result:= ch in ['0'..'9'];
end;
```

getNumber

Scanning in a number is the most involved method we'll encounter in `TScanner`. It has to identify integers, floats of the form `1.2345`, scientific notation, for example, `1.234E-4` and in the future other types of number we might want to include. Some lexical scanners pass on the string versions of these numbers to the parser. Here we will convert them to their numeric form so that this isn't something the parser has to worry about. In the process of conversion, however, we must check for arithmetic overflow and signal an error if necessary. Figure 3.6 shows the syntax diagram for a floating point number with optional scientific notation. One thing the syntax diagram doesn't address is whether a period on its own is a floating point number? Languages such as Python, or Octave treat a single period as a syntax error, we'll do the same. Likewise, the text `.E-1` will also be treated as an error. The solution is perhaps crude but we'll use two Boolean variables: `hasLeftHandSide` and `hasRightHandSide`. Each of these will be set `True` if we encounter a left or right side of a period. If neither are set `True` by the time we reach the point where we are checking for scientific notation, then we flag this as a lexical error.

The simplest operation is scanning in an integer. This is shown in the code below.

```
procedure TScanner.getNumber;
var single_digit : integer;
```

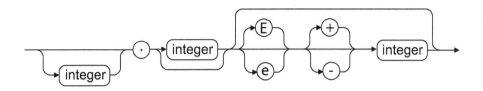

Figure 3.6 Syntax diagram for a floating point number.

```
    hasLeftHandSide, hasRightHandSide : boolean;
begin
  FTokenRecord.FTokenInteger := 0; FTokenRecord.FTokenFloat := 0.0;
  hasLeftHandSide := False; hasRightHandSide := False

  // Assume it's an integer
  FTokenRecord.FToken := tINTEGER;
  // check for decimal point just in case user has typed something like .5
  if Fch <> '.' then
     begin
     hasLeftHandSide := True;
     repeat
       singleDigit := ord (Fch) - ord ('0');
       if FTokenRecord.FTokenInteger <= (MaxInt - singleDigit) div 10 then
         begin
         FTokenRecord.FTokenInteger := 10*FTokenRecord.FTokenInteger
                    + singleDigit;
         Fch := nextchar;
         end
       else
         raise EScannerError.Create ('integer Overflow,
                 constant value too large to read');
     until not isDigit (FCh);
     end;
....
end;
```

When the scanner encounters a digit, it starts to read in the sequence of character digits that will form the integer. We must somehow convert these into a numeric value. Computing the integer value from a sequence of character digits relies on accumulating increasing powers as we read each digit. We can convert a digit character to an integer using ord (Fch) - ord ('0'). This, of course, assumes that the digit characters are contiguous on the ASCII table, which is the case. We use the following formula to accumulate a digit:

$$\text{value} = \text{value} \times 10 + \text{digit} \tag{3.1}$$

Consider reading in the integer number 25. At the start of a loop, we initialize the accumulator, FTokenInteger to zero. For the first digit, we compute the accumulated value, 0 times 10 plus the digit. This yields an accumulated value of 2. The second digit, 5, is read in and the accumulated value becomes 10*2 + 5 which yields 25. And so on if the number is larger. Each time through the loop we retrieve the next character and check it's a digit and accumulate its value.

Before we enter the loop, we also check that the first character isn't a period, '.'. This is to take into account the possibility that a user may enter something like .5 which of course isn't an integer. If this is the case, we don't attempt to read in the integer and proceed beyond this code to read in a floating point number. We also assume that when we enter the getNumber method that the type of number we'll detect will be an integer type. This is done by setting the token to tInteger. We can change this later in the method if we find we're parsing a floating point number.

As we accumulate the digits, it's possible there will be an overflow which we can handle in one of two ways. The first way is to let the runtime system signal an overflow. We just keep accumulating until the runtime system tells us we've caused an overflow. To use this method will require us to turn on the overflow directive. In Delphi we use the directive $OverFlowChecks On. The other approach is to read in the digits and add our own code to detect if we are about to exceed the numeric bounds. Integers are signed 32-bit values which have a positive maximum value of 2147483647. One more than this value and we get an overflow. Note that we don't have to deal with the possibility that the number is negative. The detection on what to do with a sign in front of the number will be handled by the parser.

Of the two approaches, we will pick the second, and not rely on the runtime system detecting the overflow. The question then remains how can we detect an overflow by code? One thing is certain, we must run the detection code before we carry out the accumulation of a digit; otherwise, it could be too late. Assume that the current value of the accumulated integer is value and that we've just read in a new digit, digit. We must make sure that before we accumulate, the following is true (see equation 3.1):

$$\text{MaxInt} \geq \text{value} \times 10 + \text{digit}$$

That is the new number must be less than the maximum possible integer, MaxInt[1]. Of course, we can't actually compute this inequality because computing the right-hand side could cause an overflow condition. Instead, let us rearrange the inequality to be (subtract Digit from both sides and divide both sides by 10):

$$(\text{MaxInt} - \text{digit}) \text{ div } 10 \geq \text{value}$$

This inequality can be safely computed without fear of an overflow condition. So long as the above inequality is true, we can accumulate the digit. The operator div represents integer division without a reminder. If the equality is false, then we raise an exception.

Once we've read in all the digits, we check whether the next character is a period or not. If we do find a period, then we are dealing with a floating point number, and we must start

---

[1]MaxInt is a built-in constant provided by the System unit.

accumulating the value to the right of the decimal point. This is easier than accumulating the left-hand side. This time instead of multiplying by 10 as each digit is collected, we divide by 10. As a result, there is no chance for an overflow condition. The code for accumulating the right-side of the decimal point is shown below:

```
scale := 1;
if Fch = '.' then
   begin
   // Then it's a float. Start collecting fractional part
   FTokenRecord.FToken := tFLOAT;
   FTokenRecord.FTokenFloat := FTokenRecord.FTokenInteger;
   Fch := nextchar;
   if isDigit (FCh) then hasRightHandSide := True;

   while isDigit (FCh) do
      begin
      scale := scale * 0.1;
      singleDigit := ord (Fch) - ord ('0');
      FTokenRecord.FTokenFloat := FTokenRecord.FTokenFloat
          + (singleDigit * scale);
      Fch := nextchar;
      end;
   end;

// Check there is actually a number
if (hasLeftHandSide = False) and (hasRightHandSide = False) then
   raise EScannerError.Create ('single period on its own is not a valid number');
```

One thing I haven't done is check that the right-hand part of the number isn't longer than 15 digits. Currently, if we do go over 15 digits, the extra digits are just ignored. In the above code there are some new variables such as `scale` and we also change the token type to a float and copy over the integer value we accumulated to `FTokenFloat`. We then retrieve the next character and start a while loop to build the right-hand side of the floating point number. Each time through the while loop we drop the `scale` value by 10 fold. If we find digits we record this fact in `hasRightHandSide`.

The last thing to do is check for scientific notation. This can apply to both integers and floats. For example, 5E2 is a valid use of scientific notation for an integer. We will cast such numbers to a floating point number as they could exceed the integer upper limit. We will allow either 'e' or 'E' to indicate the presence of scientific notation. Hence, 1.23E-2 and 1.23e-2 are both treated as numbers that use scientific notation. Once we've detected 'e' or 'E' we can read in the exponent value. This will always be an integer and less than 309 (See Chapter 2). The exponent could also be negative or positive. We must, therefore, check first for a sign and then accumulate the integer exponent.

We can use the same trick to check for overflow as we did with the integer earlier. This time the maximum integer value is 308, here called `MAX_EXPONENT` and declared at the top of the unit. The code to accumulate the exponent is shown below:

```
evalue := 0.0;
repeat
   singleDigit := ord (Fch) - ord ('0');
   if evalue <= (MAX_EXPONENT - singleDigit) div 10 then
      begin
      evalue := 10*evalue + singleDigit;
      Fch := nextchar;
      end
   else
      raise EScannerError.Create ('exponent overflow, maximum
                    value for exponent is ' + inttostr (MAX_EXPONENT));
until not isDigit (FCh);
```

The value for the exponent will be stored in `evalue`. To obtain the final number we need to raise the value we accumulated to the power of `evalue`. This is shown in the code below:

```
evalue := evalue * exponentSign;
if token = tInteger then
   FTokenRecord.FTokenFloat
      := FTokenRecord.FTokenInteger * Math.IntPower (10, evalue)
else
   FTokenRecord.FTokenFloat
      := FTokenRecord.FTokenFloat * Math.Power (10.0, evalue);
end;
```

We must remember to take into account the sign of the exponent when calculating the final value.

The `getNumber` method is perhaps a little long, and there might be a case to break it up. In addition, some functionality is repeated. For example, accumulating an integer is done twice. Breaking up the method would make even more sense if at a later stage we include other kinds of numbers and formats such as hexadecimal or octal.

For reference, the entire `getNumber` method is listed in the chapter appendix.

3.3 Our First Run

We are now ready to run our first version of the lexical analyzer. We'll create a simple console application, called `testScanner`, and use this to drive the scanner. The console application will expect a filename on the command line, something like: `testScanner test1.rh`. In order to see what file is being tested, we'll write out the contents of the test file to the console when the program starts. You can easily modify the code to read instead a string from the console if you like using `readln`.

Once the file (or string) is read in we create an instance of `TScanner` then start a while-loop to watch for `EndOfStream`. Inside the while-loop, I use a simple case statement to pick out the tokens. At the moment we can detect, identifiers, integers and strings and we ignore comments.

```
if ParamCount = 1 then
   begin
   fileName := ParamStr (1);
   writeln ('Lexical analysis of file: ', fileName);
   writeln ('Test file contents:');
   writeln ('-----------------------');
   fileContents := TFile.ReadAllText(fileName);
   writeln (fileContents);
   writeln ('-----------------------');

   sc := TScanner.create();
   try
     sc.scanString(fileContents);
     sc.nextToken;
     while sc.token <> tEndofStream do
       begin
       case sc.token of
           tIdentifier : writeln ('Identifier: ' + sc.tokenString);
           tInteger    : writeln ('Integer: ', sc.tokenInteger);
           tString     : writeln ('String: "' + sc.tokenString + '"');
       end;
       sc.nextToken;
       end;
     writeln (sLineBreak + 'Success');
     sc.Free;
   except
     on e:Exception do
       writeln (e.message);
     end;
   end
else
   writeln ('Expecting file name');

readln;
```

I also wrap the code in an exception handler to catch any lexical errors. I added a sc.Free call at the end to free the scanner. In production code, we would also wrap a try-finally around the scanner instance so that it is freed whatever happens. We can add that later on when it's more critical to do so.

This also reminds us that we haven't yet created a destructor for TScanner as we do have resources to free up. The code is shown below:

```
destructor TScanner.Destroy;
begin
  FStreamReader.Free;
  inherited Destroy;
end;
```

The final class for this version is shown below:

```
TTokenCode = (tEndOfStream);
TScanner = class (TObject)
    private
        Fch : Char;
        FColumeNumber, FLineNumber : integer;
        FTokenElement : TTokenElement;
        FStreamReader  : TStreamReader;
        procedure  startScanner;
        function   readRawChar : Char;
        function   getOS_IndependentChar : Char;
        function   nextChar : Char;
    public
        constructor Create;
        destructor  Destroy; override;
        procedure   scanString (const str : string);
        procedure   scanFile (const str : string);
        procedure   nextToken;
        property    token : TTokenCode read getTokenCode;
end;
```

3.3.1   Initial testing

At the moment we're just going to do some simple testing to make sure there isn't anything
obviously wrong with the code. In Chapter 4 we'll look at unit testing as a means to more
thoroughly test the code. To unit test we can use the DUnitX framework that comes with
Delphi. For now we'll use a series of test files and manually inspect the output. The first
test file will check that we can identify the three token types we currently support as well
as ignoring comments of the form '//'. This is shown below:

```
// test1.txt
variable // Identifier
"string" // String
12345     // Integer
```

If we run this test file we obtain on the console:

```
Identifier: variable
String: "string"
Integer: 12345
Success
```

One potentially problematic point is how the last line of the test file is terminated. There
could be newline after the last line of the file or not and it is worth testing both situations.
Here are some more tests we can try:

// test2.txt variable "string" 12345	// test3.txt variable "stri ng" "str ing"	// test4.txt "string\tTab Test"
// test5.txt /* Comment test end of comment */ variable 12345 "string"	// test6.txt "string\n\nstring"	// test7.txt 0123 00123

The problem with this type of testing is that it's difficult to ensure we have good coverage of the code-base and in this case, we manually inspect the output to check whether it is correct or not. This approach is therefore not scalable. We'll revisit testing in the next chapter when we consider unit testing.

The testing, however, is sufficient to provide a sanity check that the code is moderately in good shape. As it turns out the unit testing we do in the next chapter identified a couple of small bugs, notably that it couldn't parse numbers such as 0.5, it treated . as a zero, and it didn't correctly detect and raise an error when the source code file had CRCR, or CR (without LF) line endings. Overall there wasn't too much wrong with the code. The code you see described in this chapter is the result of running the units tests described in the next chapter.

3.4 Adding More Tokens

Currently, the scanner can identify integers, floats, strings, and identifiers. Our language however also requires us to identify a range of simple tokens such as +, - etc. and a number of keywords. The simple tokens will be handled by the one method we've not yet developed, getSpecial. This method is quite simple, and the only complication is when we have to identify compound symbols such as >=, <= and ==. The top part of getSpecial is given by the code shown below:

```
procedure TScanner.getSpecial;
begin
  case Fch of
    '+' : FTokenRecord.Ftoken := tPlus;
    '^' : FTokenRecord.Ftoken := tPower;
    '(' : FTokenRecord.Ftoken := tLeftParenthesis;
    ')' : FTokenRecord.Ftoken := tRightParenthesis;
    '[' : FTokenRecord.Ftoken := tLeftBracket;
    ']' : FTokenRecord.Ftoken := tRightBracket;
    '{' : FTokenRecord.Ftoken := tLeftCurleyBracket;
  ...
etc
```

+	tPlus		-	tMinus
*	tMult		/	tDivide
{	tLeftCurleyBracket		}	tRightCurleyBracket
(	tLeftParenthesis		)	tRightParenthesis
<	tLessThan		>	tMoreThan
<=	tLessThanOrEqual		>=	tMoreThanOrEqual
!=	tNotEqual		==	tEquivalence
;	tSemicolon		,	tComma
^	tPower			

Table 3.2 List of symbols used in Rhodus version one.

As we can see, getSpecial is one long case statement. When we identify a single character token, we assign the appropriate token code to the FTokenRecord record and fetch the next character (called at the end of the routine). Handling single character tokens is easy. For compound symbols such as >= we use the following logic.

```
'>'  : begin
       if  Char (FStreamReader.Peek) = '=' then
           begin
           Fch := nextChar;
           FTokenRecord.Ftoken := tMoreThanOrEqual;
           end
       else
           FTokenRecord.Ftoken := tMoreThan;
       end;
```

We start with a normal case identification of the first letter in the compound symbol. We then Peek to see if the next character is the equals symbol, '='. If the character is not a '=', we return the tMoreThan token. If it's a '=' we fetch the next character and assign the tMoreThanOrEqual. The same logic can be used with all the compound symbols.

If we don't identify any token in getSpecial there is an else clause that will raise an exception. This code is shown below together with the final thing we do which is to get the next character (assuming no error of course):

```
  else
     raise EScannerError.Create ('unrecognized character in source code: ' + Fch);
  end;
Fch := nextChar;
```

For version one of the Rhodus language, we will define the symbols shown in Table 3.2. With these additional tokens in place we can now tokenize input text such as:

```
x = a + 3.1415/180
y = {1,2,3,4}
```

break	if	downto	else	then
end	True	False	while	do
repeat	until	for	to	and
or	not	div	function	ref
print	println			

Table 3.3 List of reserved used in Rhodus version 1.

What we haven't implemented yet is support for keywords. These are words that have special meaning in the language, for example, `while`, `repeat` and so on. For version one, the list of reserved words is shown in Table 3.3.

One thing worth noting about this list is that I've included `True` and `False` as reserved words. This makes it much easier to identity True and False when parsing expressions. I also added `print` and `println` as keywords. We could have defined them as built-in functions but for know its easier to treat them as keywords. We'll revisit this in a later chapter.

The place to identify keywords is in the `getWord` method. Let's store the keywords in a simple `TStringList`. More seasoned developers will be thinking, why not use a dictionary? They are right, we could use a dictionary. When I wrote this code initially, I was in automatic mode and just went straight for a `TStringList`. Sometimes old habits die hard. We can revisit this in Part 2 when we'll have a chance to refactor the code. As an exercise, readers might want to refactor the code themselves and replace the `TStringList` with a `TDictionary`. In chapter 8 we will use a `TDictionary` to implement a simple symbol table.

We'll declare a variable `FKeyWords` of type `TStringList` in the `TScanner` class. In the `TScanner` constructor we'll call a method to initialize the keywords, called `addKeyWords` and in the destructor, a line will be added to free the `FKeyWords` variable. The `FKeyWords` will also be sorted so that we can use the built-in `find` method. We'll use the `TStringList` method `AddObject` to add each keyword as this allows us to associate a particular keyword with its corresponding token. This makes it convenient when it comes to searching for keywords. The method `addKeyWords` is shown below:

```
// Some predefined keywords
procedure TScanner.addKeyWords;
begin
  FKeyWordList := TStringList.Create;
  FKeyWordList.Sorted := True;

  FKeyWordList.AddObject ('if', TObject (tIf));
  FKeyWordList.AddObject ('do', TObject (tDo));
  FKeyWordList.AddObject ('to', TObject (tTo));
  FKeyWordList.AddObject ('or', TObject (tOr));
  FKeyWordList.AddObject ('end', TObject (tEnd));
  ...
```

```
etc
```

In getWord we'll add some extra lines to check if the word is a keyword or not. We'll introduce a new method called isKeyWord that will return True or False. If it returns True it also returns in an argument the corresponding token value. The updated getWord is shown below:

```
procedure TScanner.getWord;
begin
  FTokenRecord.FTokenString := '';

  while isLetter (Fch) or isDigit (Fch) do
      begin
      FTokenRecord.FTokenString := FTokenRecord.FTokenString + Fch;
      Fch := nextchar;
      end;

  if not IsKeyWord (FTokenRecord.FTokenString, FTokenRecord.FToken) then
      FTokenRecord.FToken := tIdentifier;
end;
```

The isKeyWord method is shown below. Recall that we added keywords to the list using AddObject which allows us to associate the token with the corresponding keyword. If the word is a keyword, we can return the token by accessing the Object field in the TStringList.

```
function TScanner.isKeyWord (const tokenString : string;
                       var Token : TTokenCode) : boolean;
var index : integer;
begin
  result := False;
  if FKeyWordList.Find(tokenString, index) then
      begin
      Token := TTokenCode (FKeyWordList.Objects[index]);
      exit (True);
      end;
end;
```

As mentioned at the start of this section, in Part 2 we'll probably replace the TStringList with a TDictionary which is more type-safe when retrieving the tokens.

3.5 Conclusion

This completes the first draft of the TScanner class for version one of the Rhodus language. When we get to the chapter on syntax analysis, we might find it necessary to add a few more bells and whistles, in particular, the ability to push tokens back into the scanner to assist in lookahead. This won't be difficult to do, and the changes will be minimal. With the current version of TScanner we can now write program text such as:

```
println ("Type some data")
getOut = False;
for i = 1 to 10 do
    repeat
       if i == 5 then
          getOut = True;
       end
    until getOut;
end


answer = x^2.3 + (1*y/0.12);
```

That almost looks like a real language. I updated the console application to test for the additional tokens. When we run the above test source code, we get the expected stream of tokens shown in Table 3.4.

Identifier: println	Keyword: True
Symbol: (	Keyword: ;
String: "Type some data"	Keyword: end
Symbol:)	Keyword: until
Identifier: getOut	Identifier: getOut
Symbol: Equals	Keyword: ;
Keyword: False	Keyword: end
Keyword: ;	Identifier: answer
Keyword: for	Symbol: =
Identifier: i	Identifier: x
Symbol: = Integer: 1	Symbol: power
Keyword: to	Float: 2.3
Integer: 10	Symbol: +
Keyword: repeat	Symbol: (
Keyword: if	Integer: 1
Identifier: i	Symbol: *
Symbol: ==	Identifier: y
Integer: 5	Symbol: /
Keyword: then	Float: 0.12
Identifier: getOut	Symbol:)
Symbol: =	Keyword: ;

Table 3.4 Output from the Scanner

All code can be obtained from GitHub at: https://github.com/penavon/BookPart1.

Further Reading

1. Thorsten Ball. Writing an Interpreter in GO (Date: 2017-2018)

Appendix

The getNumber method

```
procedure TScanner.getNumber;
var singleDigit : integer; scale : double;
    evalue : integer;
    exponentSign : integer;
    hasLeftHandSide, hasRightHandSide : boolean;
begin
  FTokenRecord.FTokenInteger := 0; FTokenRecord.FTokenFloat := 0.0;
  hasLeftHandSide := False; hasRightHandSide := False;

  // Assume it's an integer
  FTokenRecord.FToken := tINTEGER;
  // check for decimal point just in case user has typed something like .5
  if Fch <> '.' then
     begin
     hasLeftHandSide := True;
     repeat
       singleDigit := ord (Fch) - ord ('0');
       if FTokenRecord.FTokenInteger <= (MaxInt - singleDigit) div 10 then
          begin
          FTokenRecord.FTokenInteger
                 := 10*FTokenRecord.FTokenInteger + singleDigit;
          Fch := nextchar;
          end
       else
          raise EScannerError.Create ('integer overflow,
                 constant value too large to read');
     until not isDigit (FCh);
     end;

  scale := 1;
  if Fch = '.' then
     begin
     // Then it's a float. Start collecting fractional part
     FTokenRecord.FToken := tFLOAT; FTokenRecord.FTokenFloat
            := FTokenRecord.FTokenInteger;
     Fch := nextchar;
     if isDigit (FCh) then hasRightHandSide := True;

     while isDigit (FCh) do
        begin
        scale := scale * 0.1;
        singleDigit := ord (Fch) - ord ('0');
        FTokenRecord.FTokenFloat := FTokenRecord.FTokenFloat
               + (singleDigit * scale);
        Fch := nextchar;
        end;
```

```
      end;

  // Check there is actually a number
  if (hasLeftHandSide = False) and (hasRightHandSide = False) then
     raise EScannerError.Create ('single period on its
          own is not a valid number');


   exponentSign := 1;
  // Next check for scientific notation
  if (Fch = 'e') or (Fch = 'E') then
     begin
     // Then it's a float. Start collecting exponent part
     if FTokenRecord.FToken = tInteger then
        begin
        FTokenRecord.FToken := tFLOAT;
        FTokenRecord.FTokenFloat := FTokenRecord.FTokenInteger;
        end;
     Fch := nextchar;
     if (Fch = '-') or (Fch = '+') then
        begin
        if Fch = '-' then exponentSign := -1;
        Fch := nextchar;
        end;
     { accumulate exponent, check that first ch is a digit }
     if not isDigit (Fch) then
        raise EScannerError.Create ('syntax error:
             number expected in exponent');

     evalue := 0;
     repeat
       singleDigit := ord (Fch) - ord ('0');
       if evalue <= (MAX_EXPONENT - singleDigit) div 10 then
          begin
          evalue := 10*evalue + singleDigit;
          Fch := nextchar;
          end
       else
         raise EScannerError.Create ('exponent overflow,
                 maximum value for exponent is ' + inttostr (MAX_EXPONENT));
     until not isDigit (FCh);

     evalue := evalue * exponentSign;
     if token = tInteger then
        FTokenRecord.FTokenFloat := FTokenRecord.FTokenInteger
                   * Math.IntPower (10, evalue)
     else
        FTokenRecord.FTokenFloat := FTokenRecord.FTokenFloat
                   * Math.Power (10.0, evalue);
     end;
end;
```

4

Testing

4.1 Testing Code

In the code developed in the last chapter, I've probably committed several programming sins. For example, I wrote test code after the software was written; my testing used text files and didn't cover many cases. I also manually compared the output with the expected output, a method that doesn't scale. In this chapter, we'll consider a more scalable and systematic testing approach.

The most common methodology in use today is probably the unit test. In principle, this involves applying one or more tests to every method within a class in order to cover all possible situations. There are a number of caveats to this. First, exhaustive testing is hard to do, and secondly, we can't readily test private methods without doing some modification to the code.

There are numerous texts (see end of chapter) that describe testing, particularly unit testing and techniques such as mocking. We will focus here on how to use DUnitX that is supplied with Delphi (since Delphi 2010) to implement unit tests. Before the advent of DUnitX, Delphi developers had access to DUnit. With the advent of Generics and a much more comprehensive Rtti, DUnit was replaced with DUnitX. DUnitX itself is modeled after NUnit, with additional ideas borrowed from xUnit. Both of these are .NET unit testing frameworks.

In terms of practical testing, there seems to be considerable debate among software professionals on what to test, when to test and how to test. Some authors advocate extreme testing where virtually every line of code is tested. Others are more flexible in their approach. Within a business environment, there is often tension between testing and costs because testing is expensive. For common consumer products, a user may be willing to put up with the odd bug if it means that the costs are reduced. On the other hand, if the software is used where people's lives are at stake, for example in a hospital, then testing is of much more critical importance. There is an interesting statistic from NASA (`https://history.nasa.gov/sts1/pages/computer.html`) that claims that the development of the software aboard the Shuttle cost $1,000 per line of code ($2,400 in today's prices). This compares with $50 per line in other government software development projects. It was estimated that the shuttle software had a defect rate of 0.11 errors per 1,000 lines of code and was therefore considered, from a practical point of view, error-free. To give an example, a small to modest project might include 250,000 lines of code. By NASA's standards, testing alone would cost 6 million dollars. Presumably, the likes of NASA can justify those costs but not everyone can.

In an ideal world one would strive to test everything, but like most things in life, it isn't always possible to achieve perfection. There are, however, very sound reasons to do comprehensive testing. Probably the most useful is that a comprehensive testing suite makes it much easier to refactor or add to the code, knowing that any side effects can be quickly tested and resolved.

My personal approach is to write the application code in stages, e.g., a class with a growing list of methods. Then run basic tests on the software to make sure that the most obvious bugs are eliminated. Once most of the class is written, start writing the unit tests. The reason for this is that its likely that the requirements have been solidified to some degree at this stage. You've probably gone through a number of iterations in the code, trying different approaches. The advantage of this is that units tests can be written safe in the knowledge that the expected functionality won't likely change too much. Since unit tests tend to be hard to write and numerous, this is an advantage. The one downside is that once the software is written, many developers need herculean discipline to write the tests since it isn't the most exciting thing to do. It depends on the temperament of the developer; if you're unsure, start writing the tests immediately.

Once the unit tests are in place, the remaining bugs can be eliminated. One of the great advantages of unit testing is that we can now refractor, improve or optimize the code, knowing that any deleterious or subtle effects will be quickly identified when we rerun the unit tests. To me, this is one of the most useful aspects of unit testing and is probably a feature that is most overlooked by new developers. Uncle Bob (`https://blog.cleancoder.com/`) is a strong proponent of this idea. In the development of the lexical analyzer code, I continued to tinker with the innards of a number of methods after the unit tests had been written. In this situation, the unit tests became very useful because I could use to them to give me some assurance that I hadn't broken the code in my tinkering.

As mentioned in the last chapter, formal testing only identified a few problems and the code appeared to be in reasonable shape. The only problems identified were the inability to parse numbers such as 0.5, treating ' . ' as a zero, and it didn't correctly detect and raise an error when the source code file had CRCR, or CR (without LF) line endings.

Finally, it is worth reading a rebuttal to the unit testing argument from an essay written by James O Coplien with the title 'Why Most Unit Testing is Waste' (The reference is at the end of the chapter, together with a second installment he wrote). Unsurprisingly, the article went viral and ruffled many a feather. Some couldn't handle the arguments and resorted to personal attacks which is unfortunate as it reduces the credibility of the overall unit testing community. Unit tests certainly have a place, and as experienced in this project, they can be very useful.

4.1.1 Unit testing, what unit testing?

Now I need to own up. I don't actually do unit testing. What I actually test are expected behaviors of the class in the face of different inputs. Such tests can be designed so that they light up particular parts of the code. For example, tests that involve parsing numbers can be used to specifically target getNumber. This approach to testing is more akin to system testing. Moreover, the TScanner class has a number of private methods (such as getNumber) that are not even accessible to the DUnitX framework. Some suggest using Ifdefs to make private methods public just for the duration of the testing, but I decided against it. There are also tricks one can do with Rtti and helper methods to get access to private methods, but this is largely frowned upon for obvious reasons. I'm not even sure such trickery can be done on the latest version of Delphi. I recommend the citations at the end of the chapter for more information and some interesting discussion.

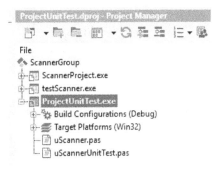

Figure 4.1 My selection of Projects in the Scanner Group. Note the ProjectUnitTest.

A significant problem is that not all methods, including the private ones, are easily testable without either redesigning the code or putting together isolation frameworks so that methods can be tested independently of the rest of the class. This could be done of course, but would involve a considerable amount of work. Some methods such as isLetter are easily tested. The only interaction between isLetter and the rest of the class is via the method call and its return value. However some methods change private variables in the class, and this would have to be simulated as well as emulating any dependencies.

There is then the issue that if the testing framework becomes complex, there is a case to put in place unit tests for the unit tests, and ad infinitum. Interestingly there were bugs in my early unit tests.

4.2   Setting up and Using DUnitX

Setting up DUnitX for testing the scanner is straightforward. Figure 4.1 shows a screenshot of my group of projects for the TScanner class. The projects include a console project, a GUI project, and a unit testing project. We need to start by creating a unit testing project within the project group.

Creating the unit testing project is made much easier if we use the DUnitX wizard. This can be started by going to File→New→Other and then select the DUnitX folder. In this folder, you'll find two file types, DUnitX Project and DUnitX Unit. Select the DUnitX Project. When selected this will bring up a simple wizard form shown in Figure 4.2. Note that DUnitX is an option when you install Delphi. If you can't find the wizard, it probably means you didn't select DUnitX when you installed Delphi. If so, reinstall Delphi.

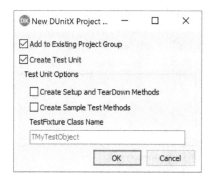

Figure 4.2 DUnitX Project Wizard

Give a name to the 'TestFixture Class Name', I happened to use TScannerTest. This is the class where all the tests will be kept. You can also select the two test unit checkboxes. Press OK to let the wizard create the project. You'll now have a new project in your group, probably called something like Project1. This will contain code to run the tests, the so-called console-runner. I would change the project name to something more suitable (right click over it and select rename) such as ProjectUnitTest. The wizard will also have created a unit1.pas which is where the tests are written. I would also rename this to something more suitable, such as uScannerUnitTests[1]. With these changes uScannerUnitTests.pas

---
[1]I tend to use a lowercase character u in front of all non-GUI units

will look like the code shown below.

```
unit uScannerUnitTests;

interface
uses
  DUnitX.TestFramework;

type

  [TestFixture]
  TScannerTest = class(TObject)
  public
    [Setup]
    procedure Setup;
    [TearDown]
    procedure TearDown;
    // Sample Methods
    // Simple single Test
    [Test]
    procedure Test1;
    // Test with TestCase Attribute to supply parameters.
    [Test]
    [TestCase('TestA','1,2')]
    [TestCase('TestB','3,4')]
    procedure Test2(const AValue1 : Integer;const AValue2 : Integer);
  end;

implementation

procedure TScannerTest.Setup;
begin
end;

procedure TScannerTest.TearDown;
begin
end;

procedure TScannerTest.Test1;
begin
end;

procedure TScannerTest.Test2(const AValue1 : Integer;const AValue2 : Integer);
begin
end;

initialization
  TDUnitX.RegisterTestFixture(TScannerTest);
end.
```

You can actually run this code, not that it will do much. If you do compile and run the code you should see the output shown below:

```
*********************************************************************
*         DUnitX - (c) 2015 Vincent Parrett & Contributors          *
*                    vincent@finalbuilder.com                       *
*                                                                   *
*         License - http://www.apache.org/licenses/LICENSE-2.0      *
*********************************************************************

DUnitX - [ProjectUnitTest.exe] - Starting Tests.


. . . . . .

Tests Found   : 3
Tests Ignored : 0
Tests Passed  : 3
Tests Leaked  : 0
Tests Failed  : 0
Tests Errored : 0
Done.. press <Enter> key to quit.
```

It claims to have found 3 tests, but these are just the stub tests that were included by the wizard. We need to add some real tests to the TScannerTest. Let's look at the TScannerTest in more detail. DUnitX relies on Delphi attributes to direct most of the action. Attributes are a way of including additional information with a given type or member of a type and can be very useful. With DUnitX, attributes are used to indicate which methods should be run to execute the tests. They are also used to indicate any methods that should be run before and after the tests are run. Traditionally these are called setup and teardown. In our case we can use setup to instantiate a TScanner object and the teardown method to free the TScanner object. This is shown in the code below:[2]

```
procedure TScannerTest.Setup;
begin
  sc := TScanner.create;
end;

procedure TScannerTest.TearDown;
begin
  sc.Free;
end;
```

The variable sc can be declared in the private area of the TScannerTest class. We are now ready to add our first test.

A test method is always proceeded with the attribute [Test] as in:

---

[2]Not everyone recommends using setup and teardown. Instead, it is recommended that each test should instantiate its own object and free it at the end.

```
[Test]
procedure TestSymbolRecognition;
```

The method can either take arguments or not as in the case above. When we run the console-runner it will locate all methods with the attribute `Test` and run them one at a time, collecting information on whether they were successful or not and printing out the results to the console.

Test methods can also take arguments; these are used when you'd like to run the same test but with many different settings (as defined by the arguments). For example, one easy test we can do is check that our scanner can identify all the reserved words and the special symbols. To set up such as test, we will create a test method that takes two arguments, an input which will be the string representing the keyword or symbol, and the expected token. Specifying the argument is done by adding additional information alongside the attribute. An example is shown below:

```
[TestCase ('TestKeyWord1', 'end,tEnd')]
```

Note that this uses the built-in keyword `TestCase` to start the attribute. There can be as many test cases as you like for a given test. In this case, the arguments include a name for the attribute, and a string containing the two arguments. DUnitX will automatically convert the arguments in the string into the appropriate type. The arguments include the input string, `"end"`, and the corresponding token that the scanner should return, in this case `tEnd`.

The test method, `TestSymbolRecognition`, is shown below:

```
procedure TScannerTest.TestSymbolRecognition (const inputString : string;
                    expectedToken : TTokenCode);
begin
  sc.scanString(inputString);
  sc.nextToken;
  Assert.AreEqual (sc.token, expectedToken);
end;
```

In this method we pass the input string, `inputString` to `scanString` and then fetch the first token. This preparatory phase is often called the 'Act' stage. After the Act stage, we are ready to run the 'Assert' phase. This is where we check that the output is what we expect. This is done using `Assert` which has a wide variety of test methods attached to it. In this case, we will use the `AreEqual` assert method. This will check whether the token is equal to the expected token.

To test the remainder of the keywords and special symbols we can write the following set of test cases for `TestSymbolRecognition`.

```
[Test] // Test Key words and specials
```

```
[TestCase ('TestKeyWord1', 'end,tEnd')]
[TestCase ('TestKeyWord2', 'while,tWhile')]
[TestCase ('TestKeyWord3', 'do,tDo')]
[TestCase ('TestKeyWord4', 'repeat,tRepeat')]
[TestCase ('TestKeyWord5', 'until,tUntil')]
[TestCase ('TestKeyWord6', 'if,tIf')]
[TestCase ('TestKeyWord7', 'then,tThen')]
[TestCase ('TestKeyWord8', '=,tEquals')]
[TestCase ('TestKeyWord10', '==,tEquivalence')]
[TestCase ('TestKeyWord9', '>,tMoreThan')]
[TestCase ('TestKeyWord10', '>=,tMoreThanOrEqual')]
[TestCase ('TestKeyWord11', '<,tLessThan')]
[TestCase ('TestKeyWord12', '<=,tLessThanOrEqual')]
[TestCase ('TestKeyWord13', '<>,tNotEqual')]
[TestCase ('TestKeyWord14', '(,tLeftParenthesis')]
[TestCase ('TestKeyWord15', '),tRightParenthesis')]
[TestCase ('TestKeyWord16', '[,tLeftBracket')]
[TestCase ('TestKeyWord17', '],tRightBracket')]
[TestCase ('TestKeyWord18', '{,tLeftCurleyBracket')]
[TestCase ('TestKeyWord19', '},tRightCurleyBracket')]
[TestCase ('TestKeyWord20', '+,tPlus')]
[TestCase ('TestKeyWord21', '-,tMinus')]
[TestCase ('TestKeyWord22', '*,tMult')]
[TestCase ('TestKeyWord23', '/,tDivide')]
[TestCase ('TestKeyWord24', '^,tPower')]
[TestCase ('TestKeyWord27', 'and,tAnd')]
[TestCase ('TestKeyWord28', 'or,tOr')]
[TestCase ('TestKeyWord27', 'not,tNot')]
[TestCase ('TestKeyWord28', 'xor,tXor')]
procedure TestSymbolRecognition (const inputString : string;
                expectedToken : TTokenCode);
```

What else can we test? We can test for overflow conditions, the different variants for floating point numbers and so on. The tests for the floating point numbers are shown below:

```
[Test] // Floating point numbers
[TestCase ('TestFloat1', '3.1415,3.1415,tFloat')]
[TestCase ('TestFloat2', '0.1415,0.1415,tFloat')]
[TestCase ('TestFloat3', '.5,0.5,tFloat')]
[TestCase ('TestFloat4', '1E-1,0.1,tFloat')]
[TestCase ('TestFloat5', '1E+1,10,tFloat')]
[TestCase ('TestFloat6', '1E-3,0.001,tFloat')]
[TestCase ('TestFloat6', '1.234E-3,0.001234,tFloat')]
[TestCase ('TestFloat7', '0.234E-3,0.000234,tFloat')]
procedure TestFloatingPoint (const Value1 : string; Value2 : double;
            token : TTokenCode);
```

Here are the integer tests:

```
[Test] // Integer values
[TestCase ('TestInteger1', '25,25,tInteger')]
```

```
[TestCase ('TestInteger2', '0,0,tInteger')]
[TestCase ('TestInteger3', '0123,123,tInteger')]
procedure TestIntegerScanning (const Value1 : string; Value2 : integer;
          Value3 : TTokenCode);
```

Testing Exceptions

The integer overflow tests are separate because we have to show that an exception is raised. This is done with the assert method `WillRaise`. For example, the integer overflow test declaration is given by:

```
[Test] // Integer Overflow
[TestCase ('TestIntOverflow', '2147483648')] // 2147483647 is transition
procedure TestIntOverflow (const Value1 : string);
```

The body of `TestIntOverflow` is given as follows:

```
procedure TScannerTest.TestIntOverflow (const Value1 : string);
begin
  sc.scanString(Value1);
  Assert.WillRaise(procedure begin sc.nextToken; end, EScannerError,
          'Int Overflow Raised');
end;
```

The method `WillRaise` takes three arguments. The third argument is a simple string message and the second argument is the excepted exception that will be handled. The most interesting part is the first argument which is a reference to a Procedure. The declaration of `WillRaise` is:

```
class procedure Assert.WillRaise(const AMethod : TTestLocalMethod;
          const exceptionClass : ExceptClass; const msg : string);
```

where you can see the three different arguments. The first argument, of type `TTestLocal-Method`, is defined as:

```
TTestLocalMethod = reference to procedure;
```

The `reference to procedure` type was introduced in Delphi 2010 and can be used to reference anonymous methods. Such methods are just chunks of code of the form:

```
procedure (optional arguments) begin code here end;
```

Note that the anonymous method doesn't have a name, hence anonymous method. AMethod is, therefore, an anonymous method. In this case an anonymous method that takes no arguments. This means we can call `WillRaise` as follows:

```
Assert.WillRaise(procedure begin sc.nextToken; end, EScannerError,
                 'Int Overflow Raised');
```

The anonymous method is defined as procedure begin sc.nextToken; end. The assert will run this anonymous method and assert true if an exception of the type TScanner-Error is invoked.

The following tests check that the scanner will raise exceptions for malformed numbers:

```
[Test]
procedure TestMissingExponent;
[Test]
procedure TestExponentOverflow;
[Test]
procedure TestExponentPeriod;
```

We also check for a variety of good and bad line endings and ensure that exceptions are raised in the bad line endings:

```
[Test] // Filter CRLF
[TestCase ('TestCRLF1', 'before'+sLineBreak+'after,before,after')]
[TestCase ('TestCRLF2', 'before'+#10+'after,before,after')]
[TestCase ('TestCRLF3', 'before'+#10#10+'after,before,after')]
[TestCase ('TestCRLF4', 'before'+#10#10#10+'after,before,after')]
procedure TestCRLF (const Value1, Value2, Value3 : string);

[Test] // Filter CRLF Exception Test, CR on its own
[TestCase ('TestCRLFExc', 'before'+#13+'after')]
procedure TestCRLFException1 (const Value1 : string);

[Test] // Filter CRLF Exception Test, multiple CFs
[TestCase ('TestCRLFExc', 'before'+#13#13+'after')]
procedure TestCRLFException2 (const Value1 : string);

[Test] // Filter CRLF Exception Test, multiple CFs
[TestCase ('TestCRLFExc', 'before'+#13#13#13+'after')]
procedure TestCRLFException3 (const Value1 : string);
```

Finally here are a number of miscellaneous tests including comments, escape characters, illegal characters, and others.

```
// Test sequence of tokens
[Test]
procedure TestSequenceOfTokens;

[Test] // Use of \t in strings
procedure TestTabKeyInString;

[Test] // Use of \n\n in string
procedure TestTwoNewlinesInString;
```

```
[Test] // Comment test: // Comment [No newline]
procedure TestOneLineCommentWithoutNewLine;

[Test]   // Comment test: // Comment [With newline]
procedure TestOneLineComment;

[Test]   // Comment test: /* Comment */
procedure TestMultiLineCommentOnSameLine;

[Test]   // Comment test: /* Comment [newline] Comment */
procedure TestMultiLineCommentOnMultipleLines;

[Test]    // Test for illegal character exception
procedure TestIllegalCharacter;

[Test]    // Test for MALFORMED !=
procedure TestNotEqualsToError;

[Test]   // Test for "String
procedure TestUnterminatedString;

[Test]    // Test for /* Fiish me
procedure TestUnterminatedComment;
```

The last two tests to put in included tests to check that unterminated strings and comments would raise an appropriate exception. This is the list of tests at the time of publication. There could well be additional tests in the source code on GitHub since publication.

One thing to mention is that the tests didn't just appear all at once but grew over time, and even when I thought I was done, I came up with some unusual edge cases to test. Testing is therefore never quite done, and the idea of doing a full and comprehensive test system is probably unattainable especially for a complex system.

```
****************************************************************
*      DUnitX - (c) 2015 Vincent Parrett & Contributors      *
*              vincent@finalbuilder.com                      *
*                                                            *
*      License - http://www.apache.org/licenses/LICENSE-2.0  *
****************************************************************

DUnitX - [ProjectDUnitXTest.exe] - Starting Tests.

.............................................................

Tests Found   : 70
Tests Ignored : 0
Tests Passed  : 70
Tests Leaked  : 0
Tests Failed  : 0
```

```
Tests Errored : 0
Done.. press <Enter> key to quit.
```

4.2.1   Other useful assert methods

Table 4.1 shows a list of assert methods that I obtained from the Embarcadero web site under "DUnitX Overview" as well as some additional ones listed on the DUnitX GitHub page.

Function	Description
Pass	Checks that a routine works.
Fail	Checks that a routine fails.
AreEqual	Checks to see if items are equal.
AreNotEqual	Checks to see if items are not equal.
AreSame	Checks to see that two items have the same value.
AreNotSame	Checks to see that two items do not have the same value.
Contains	Checks to see if the item is in a list.
DoesNotContain	Checks to see if the item is not in a list.
IsTrue	Checks that a condition is true.
IsFalse	Checks that a condition is false.
IsEmpty	Checks to see if the value of an item is empty.
IsNotEmpty	Checks to see if the value of an item is not empty.
IsNull	Checks to see that an item is null.
IsNotNull	Checks to see that an item is not null.
WillRaise	Checks to see if the method will raise an exception.
StartsWith	Checks if a string starts with a specified substring.
EndsWith	Checks if a string ends with a specified substring.
InheritsFrom	Checks if a class is descendant of a specified class.
IsMatch	Checks if the item matches with a specified pattern.

Table 4.1 List of other Assert methods available with DUnitX.

4.2.2   Final remarks

It's impossible to prove in general and in the mathematical sense, that a piece of software is bug-free. Instead, the degree of testing provides a level of confidence in the reliability of the software. The more testing, the higher the level of confidence. Given what tests were done on the lexical analyzer, I am confident that the code is relatively bug-free and appears to perform its intended purpose.

You can find a useful discussion on these more philosophical issues at a StackOverflow `https://goo.gl/UPE1ab` to the question: "is it possible to reach absolute zero bug state for large-scale software".

Further Reading

1. Thorsten Ball. Writing an Interpreter in GO (Date: 2017-2018)

2. Nick Hodges. Coding in Delphi. Nepeta Enterprises (2014) ISBN-13: 978-1941266038

3. Roy Oshrove. The Art of Unit Testing: with examples in C#, Manning Publications; Second edition (December 7, 2013) ISBN-13: 978-1617290893

4. Robert C. Martin (aka. Uncle Bob), The Clean Code Blog https://blog.cleancoder.com/

5. James O Coplien. Why Most Unit Testing is Waste (2014), https://rbcs-us.com/documents/Why-Most-Unit-Testing-is-Waste.pdf

6. James O Coplien. Seque https://rbcs-us.com/documents/Segue.pdf

7. Mock Object. https://en.wikipedia.org/wiki/Mock_object

8. What is Mocking? https://stackoverflow.com/questions/2665812/what-is-mocking

Access to Private Fields: The bottom line is don't do it.

1. Access a strict protected property of a Delphi class? (2011) https://stackoverflow.com/questions/8330003/access-a-strict-protected-property-of-a-delphi-class/8330615#8330615

2. Hallvard Vassbotn, Hack #5: Access to private fields (2004) http://hallvards.blogspot.com/2004/06/hack-5-access-to-private-fields.html

3. Marco Cantu, Closing the Class Helpers Private Access Loophole (2016) https://goo.gl/4bV7fs

4. Nick Hodges, Delphi Unit Tests / Accessing Private Members (2013) at Bitbucket: https://goo.gl/VvJg1N

5

An Interactive Console

5.1 Creating a REPL

REPL stands for "Read Eval Print Loop". If you've used something like Python, or R you'll be familiar with a REPL. A REPL allows you to 'talk' to your interpreter in an interactive way and very often in real-time. This is one of the key differences that distinguishes a compiler from an interpreter.

At the moment our interpreter doesn't do much, but we could write a REPL that accepts source code and prints out the tokens. Not very exciting perhaps but this can form the basis of a more sophisticated REPL later on. It can also provide a convenient place to try out new functionality before writing unit tests.

We can start by creating a new project within our existing group. We'll create a console based project which we can call `REPL_Project_LexicalConsole`. What might interaction with the REPL be like? Below is something we might want to emulate:

```
Welcome to the Rhodus Lexical Analysis Console, Version 0.1,
Nov 29, 2018, 12.05am
>> a = 3.14
```

When Rhodus starts we can write a welcome message, output a prompt and wait for input. It might also be worth writing out the current version in addition to the current date and time.

5.2   Implementing the REPL

You may have observed that when you run a console window, the window will close in a puff of smoke once all input has been accepted. As a personal preference, the first thing I tend to do when starting to write a console application is add a `readln` at the very end so that this doesn't happen. So that the user isn't too confused, we'll also add a message saying `'Press any key to exit'`. The first iteration of the REPL will look like:

```
begin
  writeln ('Press any key to exit');
  readln;
end;
```

The next thing is to declare some variables; these include a reference to the lexical analyzer object and a place to put the source code we obtain from the user.

```
var sourceCode : string;
    sc : TScanner;
```

The next thing is to create an instance of the scanner itself. This time we'll use a `try/fin-ally` to ensure that the scanner reference is also freed no matter what happens. I also added a `displayWelcome` call when the REPL first starts up. The code now looks like:

```
begin
  sc := TScanner.Create;
  try
    displayWelcome;

    ... the rest of the code goes here

    writeln ('Press any key to exit');
    readln;
  finally
    sc.Free;
  end;
end;
```

The following might not be to everyone's taste, but I'm going to start a `while True` loop that's going to read, interpret and output the results. I'm going to check if the user typed in `quit`, and if so I will `break` the `while` loop. Here is the code with the `while` loop added:

```
begin
  sc := TScanner.Create;
  try
    displayWelcome;
    while True do
      begin
```

```
      ... the rest of the code goes here
        end;
    writeln ('Press any key to exit');
    readln;
  finally
    sc.Free;
  end;
end;
```

Once inside the `while` loop, the first thing to do is issue a prompt by calling `displayPrompt`. This method is shown below:

```
procedure displayPrompt;
begin
  write ('>> ');
end;
```

We then store in the variable `sourceCode`, whatever the user typed at the keyboard. This approach means we're taking user input one line at a time with a newline indicating the end of the user input. At this point, we can check if the user typed `quit` and if they did we `break`. This leads to:

```
1   begin
2     sc := TScanner.Create;
3     try
4       displayWelcome;
5       while True do
6         begin
7         displayPrompt;
8         readln (sourceCode);
9         if sourceCode = 'quit' then
10            break;
11          ... the rest of the code goes here
12          end;
13
14      writeln ('Press any key to exit');
15      readln;
16    finally
17      sc.Free;
18    end;
19  end;
```

Now we come to call the interpreter. Just after the `break` statement on line 11 we'll add the following code:

```
  sc.scanString(sourceCode); ;
  try
      sc.nextToken;
      while sc.token <> tEndofStream do
```

```
            begin
            writeln (sc.tokenToString);
            sc.nextToken
            end;
       except
         on e:exception do
            writeln ('Error: ' + e.Message);
       end;
```

This code will load the source code into the scanner, fetch the first token and start a
`while` loop that checks if the most recent token is not `tEndOfStream`. If the token isn't a
`tEndOfStream` we enter the body of the `while` loop and call a new method we've not seen
before, `tokenToString` followed by retrieving a new token. After the `scanString` call
we'll also wrap the code in a `try/except` to catch any lexical errors. The final result is the
following code:

```
begin
  sc := TScanner.Create;
  try
    displayWelcome;
    while True do
        begin
        displayPrompt;
        readln (sourceCode);
        if sourceCode = 'quit' then
            break;

        sc.scanString(sourceCode); ;
        try
          sc.nextToken;
          while sc.token <> tEndofStream do
              begin
              writeln (sc.tokenToString);
              sc.nextToken
              end;
        except
          on e:exception do
              writeln ('Error: ' + e.Message);
        end;
        end;

    writeln ('Press any key to exit');
    readln;
  finally
    sc.Free;
  end;
end;
```

Before continuing, I should mention `tokenToString`[1]. This method will convert the current token into a human-readable string. It's only really useful for debugging purposes as its unlikely we'll need this for anything else. The top part of the method is shown below:

```
function TScanner.TokenToString : string;
begin
  case token of
    tIdentifier : result := 'identifier <' + FTokenElement.FTokenString + '>';
    tInteger    : result := 'integer <'+inttostr (FTokenElement.FTokenInteger)+'>';
    tFloat      : result := 'float <'+floattostr (FTokenElement.FTokenFloat)+'>';
    tString     : result := 'string "' + FTokenElement.FTokenString + '"';
    tMinus      : result := 'special: ''-''';
    tPlus       : result := 'special: ''+''';
    tMult       : result := 'special: ''*''';
    tDivide     : result := 'special: ''/''';
    tPower      : result := 'special: ''^''';
    etc
```

The method is one big case statement. There is a small `else` provision at the end:

```
else
  result := 'unrecognised token in tokenToString: ' + inttostr (integer(token));
end;
```

which proved very useful to catch tokens I hadn't properly dealt with.

I also added a version constant:

```
const
  RHODUS_VERSION = '1.0';
```

and the welcome method. The welcome method can be modified to whatever you'd like:

```
procedure displayWelcome;
begin
  writeln ('Welcome to Rhodus, Version ', RHODUS_VERSION);
  writeln ('Data and Time: ', dateToStr (Date), ', ', timeToStr (Time));
end;
```

If we run the REPL the output below is typical:

```
Welcome to the Rhodus Lexical Analysis Console, Version 1.0
Data and Time: 12/1/2018, 10:02:22 AM
>> a = 1
identifier <a>
special: '='
```

---

[1]I could have called the method `toString` which is more in line with this kind of method but chose `tokenToString` to be more explicit for the reader.

```
integer <1>
>> while time < 60 do
key word: <while>
identifier <time>
special: '<'
integer <60>
key word: <do>
>> quit
Press any key to exit
```

That completes the REPL, at least for now.

Further Reading

1. Thorsten Ball. Writing an Interpreter in GO (Date: 2017-2018)

6

Introduction to Syntax Analysis

6.1 Introduction

And now for some theory. In this chapter I'm going to talk a little bit about syntax analysis. We won't go too deeply into it, just enough to help you understand the basics of language parsing. This is an important topic that will prepare us for the next part of our interpreter which is checking that the tokens we retrieve from the lexical scanner are arranged in ways that make grammatical sense. For example, the following statement in Rhodus does not make any sense:

```
a 5 =
```

The question is, how do we write software to tell us that?

We need to somehow represent the series of tokens in a way that reflects the syntax of the source code. This will allow us to further analyze the text and ultimately use it to generate executable code. It turns out that a very convenient way to represent the syntax is through a syntax tree structure. We will delve more deeply into syntax trees later.[1]

6.2 Grammar

Let's begin with what we mean by a grammar. A grammar is a set of rules that allow us to specify how to form sentences in a language. In computer science, a convenient notation

---

[1]The code for this chapter can be found in GitHub in the Calculator_Chapr6 folder.

for describing these rules is the Extended Backus-Naur Form or EBNF. Let's start with a very simple example. Let's say our entire language describes a simple assignment, for example:

$$a = 2 \tag{6.1}$$

We'd like to construct a grammar rule that will help us decide whether our sentence is valid or not. The first thing we do is split the symbols of the language into two kinds:

terminal and **non-terminal**

The terminal symbols are the most elementary symbols in the language. In our example these will include: a, =, and 2. The terminal symbols are in fact the tokens we get from the lexical analyzer. The non-terminal symbols are the high-level constructs in our language. In our simple language, there is only one high-level construct, and that is the assignment. In more complicated languages there will be many high-level constructs.

EBNF is used to describe a language in terms of grammar rules, or more specifically called **production rules**.

> A production rule describes how a non-terminal can be written in terms of other terminals and non-terminals.

A production rule will have the structure:

```
non-terminal = one or more terminals and non-terminals
```

Strictly speaking, production rules are replacement rules, also known as rewrite rules. A production rule will replace whatever is on the left with whatever we have on the right. For example

```
A = B
```

means that A can be replaced with B. Or:

```
A = BC
```

means whenever we see A, we can replace it with the two symbols B and C. The complete syntax for a language is described by a set of such production rules. The symbol = is standard notation in EBNF for separating the right from the left side of a production rule though many authors will use the symbol : := instead. However, the ISO standard states that = is the correct separator. Personally, I prefer : :=, but we'll use the recommended symbols.

In principle, it's possible to have no terminals or non-terminals on the right-hand side. This would mean we replace the non-terminal with nothing; this isn't something we come across in this book.

Before proceeding further, we should point out that there are a number of different classes of grammars. The class of grammar used to describe programming languages is called a **context-free grammar**. A context-free grammar is where the left-hand side of a production rule **only** contains a **single** non-terminal, and the right-hand side can contain any number of non-terminals or terminals. There are also context-sensitive grammars, where there may be multiple symbols on the left-hand side. In this book, we'll only work with context-free grammars.

The two important rules to remember that apply to a context-free grammar are:

> 1. The left-hand side of a production rule will only contain a **single** non-terminal.

> 2. The right-hand side can contain terminals and non-terminals.

There are two ways we can use a grammar. On the one hand, we can use it to generate sentences consistent with the grammar, or we can do the reverse and try to determine whether a given sentence is consistent with the grammar (Figure 6.1).

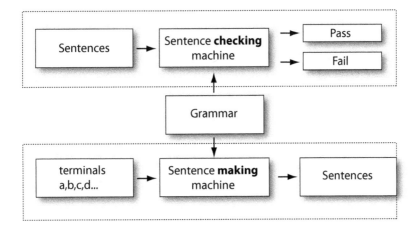

Figure 6.1 Grammar Machines: Creating or Checking Sentences.

Generating sentences from a grammar is straightforward. Consider the production rule:

A = a | aA

where a is a terminal and A a non-terminal.

> In general lower case letters will be used to denote terminals, and uppercase letters to denote non-terminals.

We've also introduced a new symbol, the vertical bar, '|'. It can be translated to mean OR. Hence the production rules says we can replace the non-terminal A with either a OR aA.

The symbol '|' represents alternatives, that is OR.

To generate sentences, we repeatedly apply the rule. We continue to apply the rule until the resulting sentence is only composed of terminals. For example, one possible sentence using our example is 'a' which we obtained by applying A = a. Since the sentence only contains terminals, we stop. However, if we choose the other option in the grammar, we obtain aA. Since this contains a non-terminal, we must continue. One possibility is to replace the A in aA with 'a' so that the sentence becomes aa. With only terminals in the sentence, we stop. It's not difficult to work out many other valid sentences such as aaa, aaaa, and so on. In fact, an infinite number of sentences can be generated from this grammar. The reason for this is that the grammar is recursive, that is 'A' appears on both sides of the production rule. Not all grammars are like this, some grammars will generate a finite number of sentences. For example, consider the following grammar:

```
S = A
A = aB | BBb
B = b | ab
```

a and b are the terminals and S, A, and B are the non-terminals. This grammar will generate a finite number of sentences that include ab, aab, bbb, babb, abbb, ababb. These are the only sentences that are consistent with this grammar.

In any grammar, there will also be a non-terminal that represents the **start symbol** of the grammar. We will sometimes use the non-terminal, program to represent the start non-terminal otherwise the start symbol tends to be denoted by S. The start non-terminal is the highest construct of all within the language.

6.2.1 Testing sentences against a grammar

A more important question for parsing computer languages is to ask the opposite to what we just did. That is, given a sentence how can we decide that the sentence is consistent with a given grammar (Figure 6.1). This is precisely the question we have to address in writing a parser for a computer language.

Production rules describe a language in a top-down fashion by looking at higher-level constructs first then drilling down to simpler constructs until we eventually reach the terminal symbols. Consider the production rule for a simple assignment:

```
assignment = variable '+' integer
```

Because there is only a single production rule the non-terminal assignment is the start symbol. The rule states that an assignment is a variable followed by a plus symbol followed by an integer. One of the huge advantages of using production rules is that we can convert them into software. This is done by creating a method whose name is the non-terminal on the left of the production rule, and the body of the method represents the right-hand side of the production rule. An example might make this clearer. Using the assignment rule above we can represent it in software as follows:

```
procedure assignment;
begin
  expect (tIdentifier);
  expect (tEquals);
  expect (tInteger);
end
```

The method expect reads 'expect the token given in the argument'. It checks that the token we are looking for is next in the input stream. The code for expect would be something like:

```
procedure expect (expectedToken : TTokenCode);
begin
  if sc.token = expectedToken then
     sc.nextToken
  else
     raise ESyntaxError.Create('expecting: ' + sc.tokenToString (expectedToken));
end;
```

We'll assume that sc is a reference to a TScanner object. If at any time the expect method fails we know that our sentence is not consistent with the grammar and we therefore raise an exception. For example, the sentence a 5 = would fail to parse correctly when we call assignment. You'll find expect like procedures in most interpreters and compilers. They're called various names such as eat, checkfor or match.

The method also introduces the syntax exception, ESyntaxException. This is defined simply as:

ESyntaxError = class (Exception)

The method assignment is our first syntax parser.

Summary:

Let's reflect on what we did here. We created a method directly from the production rule. We named the method using the same name as the non-terminal on the left side and then implemented the right-hand side in the body of the method. This is going to be a pattern we will use again and again.

6.3 Production Rules

Let's look in more detail at production rules. EBNF defines a number of syntactic elements to describe different scenarios. We've already seen two; the sequence and the alternative. We can combine both these forms into the following production rule:

```
A = B1 B2 ...| C1 C2 ...| D1 D2 ...
```

As mentioned before the | symbol is read as OR. A real example that uses alternatives is the definition of a digit:

```
digit = 0 | 1 | 2 | 3 | 4 | 5 | 6 | 7 | 8 | 9
```

This reads a digit is a 0 or a 1 or 2 etc. Productions can also be recursive such as:

```
A = y | xA
```

Note that the non-terminal A is also on the right-hand side. We saw this construction in a previous example. As we'll shortly see, if the non-terminal were on the left, such as A = A x, there will be problems when we try to implement the production in software. The other common construct is repetition. For that, EBNF uses curly brackets. For example[2]:

```
P = A { BC }
```

This rule tells use that a valid sentence, P, is A followed by **zero** or more pairs of the BC construct.

6.3.1 Checking a sentence against a grammar

Imagine we have a set of production rules as follows:

```
S = R | aSc
R = c | bR
```

Consider the input string 'abbcc'.

Let's use the production rules to decide if this is a valid sentence or not. As before capitals denote non-terminals and lower case terminals. Recall that for abstract examples such as this, it is common to use the symbol S to indicate the starting non-terminal. Remember that if we see something like aSc it means the sequence a followed by S, followed by c. The process by which we work through a set of production rules to arrive at the input string is called a **derivation** and there are systematic ways to carry this out. We will use a technique called **left-derivation**. This means that each time we apply a rule, we will apply it to the leftmost non-terminal[3] first.

---

[2]Another common but unofficial notation for repetition is (BC)*
[3]There is also a right-derivation, but we won't worry about that here.

> **Definition:**
>
> **Left-derivation**: A left-derivation is obtained when the leftmost non-terminal is re-placed at each application of a production.
>
> **Right-derivation**: A right-derivation is obtained when the rightmost non-terminal is replaced at each application of a production.

We begin with the start symbol S. The right-hand side of the production rule for the start symbol is R | aSc. There are two options, the first option is R and the second one is aSc, Because the first token in abbcc is 'a' we pick the second option to give us aSc. This is often denoted by:

S ⇒ aSc

This reads: S is **replaced** by aSc. The intermediate forms such as aSc are often called **sententials**. The next step is to apply a production rule to the sentential aSc. With left-derivation we must always choose to replace the left-most non-terminal. In this case the left-most non-terminal in aSc is S. Note that there is only one non-terminal so there isn't much of a choice. This means we again have to choose between R and aSc and since the second token in the input string is 'b' we will pick the first choice R because it can't possibly be aSc. This yields:

S ⇒ aSc ⇒ aRc

As a reminder, this means aSc is replaced with aRc. The left-most non-terminal in aRc is now R. For R we have two choices, 'c' or bR. Since the second token in abbcc is 'b' we pick the second option. We replace the left-most non-terminal, R with bR to yield:

S ⇒ aSc ⇒ aRc ⇒ abRc

The left-most non-terminal in abRc is again R and again we have two choices for R, either 'c' or bR. Since the third token in abbcc is 'b' we pick bR, this yields:

S ⇒ aSc ⇒ aRc ⇒ abRc ⇒ abbRc

The left-most non-terminal is again R. Since the fourth token in abbcc is 'c' we pick the first option in the second production to obtain:

S ⇒ aSc ⇒ aRc ⇒ abRc ⇒ abbRc ⇒ abbcc

Because the final sentence has no more non-terminals, the derivation is complete, and we confirm that 'abbcc' is a valid sentence based on the production rules.

In doing this exercise, we had to carefully choose the production rule each time. If we couldn't proceed, i.e., we couldn't make a replacement, then this would signal a syntax error. In other words, we would say that the input string is not consistent with the grammar.

6.4 Recursive Descent

The approach we just used to figure out whether a given sentence is consistent with a grammar or not can easily be implemented in software. It's a technique called **recursive descent**. It's called recursive because we might have a situation where a production rule refers to itself on the left-hand side or via other production rules. The descent part relates to the fact that recursive descent starts at the highest order construct and works its way to simpler and simpler constructs until to reaches the terminal symbols.[4] This is called a top-down approach which suggests there are also bottom-up approaches which is true, but we won't be concerned with those in this book.

6.4.1 Implementation

In software, recursive descent is implemented by writing a method for each production rule. In the case of the assignment rule, the assignment method was quite simple, we just had to check that the sequence of terminals was an identifier, followed by an equals sign followed by a number. In a more complicated grammar, we'll be making other kinds of decisions according to the particular production rule. Luckily there are only a limited number of patterns to deal with when it comes to production rules. For example, choices that are based on the OR operator '|' can either be handled by `if` or a `case` statement and repetitions can be handled by `while` loops. If we're expecting specific terminals, we can check for those with a simple `if` statement. Let's convert the two productions in the most recent example into software.

Because there were two non-terminals, there will be two methods, called S and R. We can write the S method as follows:

```
// S = R | aSc
procedure S;
begin
   if sc.token = a then
      begin
      sc.nextToken;
      S();
      expect (c);
      end
   else
      R();
end
```

It is common practice to add the production rule as a comment at the start of the procedure. We check for the terminal 'a', if we don't find 'a' then we must use the alternative, R and

---

[4]More accurately it relates to the fact that parsing results in a tree that represents the parsed language and the tree will grow from the root 'downwards' towards the leaves.

so we call R(). If we do find 'a' we proceed to get the next token, call S and expect 'c' to follow. The method for the non-terminal R is given below:

```
// R = c | bR
procedure R;
begin
   if sc.token = b then
      begin
      sc.nextToken;
      R();
      end
   else
      expect (c);
end
```

We check if the token is 'b', if it is we must choose bR which means retrieve the next token and call R(). If not we just expect 'c'. We could also have initially tested for 'c' instead, it makes no difference in this case. With a valid input string such as abbbc the parsing should succeed.

6.4.2 Parsing arithmetic

Let's now consider a more practical example by extending the assignment to include simple addition expressions on the right-hand side. For example the following will be valid sentences in the new language:

```
a = 2
b = 4 + 5
b = a
a = a + b
b = a + 2
x = a + b + c + ...
```

If you think about it, there are an infinite number of possible valid sentences in this language because we allow sentences such as x = a + b + c + ... so there is probably going to be some level of recursion in the grammar.

As before we'll set the start non-terminal to be the assignment. The terminal symbols are the same except for the new plus symbol:

```
terminals = ( identifier, integer, equals, plus )
```

Let's write out the production rules for this new language:

```
assignment = variable '=' expression
expression = term { '+' term }
term       = integer | variable
```

(6.2)

Usage	Notation
definition	=
alternation		
repetition	{ ... }
optional	[..]
grouping	(...)
empty set	ϵ

Table 6.1 A summary of some of the notation used in EBNF.

To describe the structure of our language, we're using alternatives and repetition in the production rules. We've created two new non-terminals, that is higher-level constructs: expression and term.

The start production rule, assignment, tells us that an assignment is a variable followed by equals followed by the non-terminal expression. Since expression is a non-terminal it must have its own production rule. The expression production rule uses a repetition by stating that an expression is a term followed by **zero** or more groups of ('+' term). The use of repetition allows the following sentence to be a grammatically correct in our language:

a = 2 + 3 + 4

term is also a non-terminal so it must also have its own production rule. In this case, we use an alternative rule to describe a term. A term is either a variable or an integer. In other words either something like abc or 123.

Strictly speaking both variable and integer are not terminal symbols because we know they are made up of even smaller components, letters and digits. However our lexical analyzer has already dealt with these and so we're receiving integers and variables from the lexical scanner as if there were terminals. In the full grammar specification, we would also describe variables and integers. In Chapter 3 we actually did do this in the form of railroad diagrams.

For completeness we can define a variable and integer in the following form using EBNF:

```
digit    = '0' | '1' | '2' | '3' | '4' | '5' | '6' | '7' | '8' | '9'
letter   = 'a' | 'b' | ... | 'A' | 'B' | ... | '_'
integer  = [ '-' ] digit { digit }
variable = letter { letter | digit }
```

Here we've introduced another new EBNF notation; anything in square brackets, such as ['-'] is optional. Table 6.1 summarizes all the EBNF symbols we've used except for grouping and the empty set. Appendix A describes EBNF in more detail.

Let's convert the EBNF production rules (6.2) into source code. Let's start with the production rule that describes a term. Since we're looking for either an integer or a variable, we can use a case statement. If we find neither, then we raise an error. Note that each time we recognize a terminal, be it an integer or variable, we also fetch the next token. In fact, there is a general rule here:

> Each time we identify a terminal symbol we call `nextToken`.

Here is the code for the production rule that defines `term`:

```
// Parse rule: term = integer | variable
procedure term;
begin
  case token of
     tInteger:   sc.nextToken;
     tIdentifier: sc.nextToken;
  else
     raise ESyntaxError.Create ('Expecting integer or variable in term');
  end;
end;
```

Notice that when we identify the terminals `tInteger` or `tIdentifer` we call `nextToken`.

The other non-terminal we must define is the `expression` production rule. It's a little bit more involved but still straightforward. The code is given by:

```
// Parse rule: expression = term { '+' term }
procedure expression;
begin
  term;
  while token = tPlus then
     begin
     sc.nextToken;
     term;
     end;
end;
```

We first call `term`. We expect that when `term` returns, the next token has been fetched since `term` will have eventually drilled down to a terminal symbol. We note from the production rule that there could be a set of repeated symbols of the form `'+' term`. We can check to see if the next token is a plus and if it is, we retrieve the next token and call `term`. Since the pattern `'+' term` can be repeated, we use a `while` loop to keep checking for a plus until we find none. Table 6.2 summarizes the common production rule patterns together with the corresponding Object Pascal code.

This seems straightforward, once we have the production rules in place, it doesn't seem that difficult to convert them into real code. Because parsing can be formalized, there are in fact automated applications such as Yacc (yet another compiler compiler) and ANTLR (ANother Tool for Language Recognition) that will read specific production rule languages and automatically create a parser although they tend to use alternative parsing approaches based on tables.

EBNF	Equivalent Object Pascal Code
Pattern	`except(terminal)`
A | B | C	```case token of A() : B() : C() : else raise ESyntaxError ('Error');```
A { '*' A }	```A(); while (token = '*') do begin sc.nextToken; A(); end;```
[a]	```if sc.token = a then begin sc.nextToken; end;```

Table 6.2 Production rules and corresponding Object Pascal code.

At this point, we actually have enough information to write a full parser. As a result, the next section is optional. It covers some of the problems that one can encounter when designing a grammar and how to fix them. Assuming your grammar is good to go, you can jump straight to the section beyond which starts development of a simple calculator.

6.5 Restrictions of Context-Free Grammars (Optional)

There are some restrictions to a recursive descent parser, but most of these can be avoided by careful design of the production rules. Three major issues include:

1. Identical choices between two productions, meaning we can't make a unique decision (left factoring).

2. The possibility of going into an infinite loop (left recursion).

3. A grammar that is ambiguous, meaning that there is more than one way to interpret the grammar (ambiguity).

Summary:

A Context Free Grammar Consists of:

Terminal Symbols: These are the lowest elements of the language. From a programming perspective, they are the tokens retrieved from the lexical analyzer.

Non-terminals Symbols: These are higher level constructs in the language that are built from terminals and/or other high-level non-terminal constructs.

Production Rules: These are rules for replacing non-terminal symbols with other non-terminal or terminal symbols.

Left-side of a production rule: The left-side of a production will have a single non-terminal.

Right-side of a production rule: The right-side of a production will have zero or more terminals and non-terminals.

Start Symbol: The start symbol, often labeled S, can be thought of as the highest construct in the language and is where parsing will begin.

We'll briefly cover these three issues here. Since the grammar we'll use for Rhodus will generally not have any of these problems, readers can skip to the next section if they'd like to get started on programming a simple calculator.

6.5.1   LL(k)

In an ideal recursive descent parser, we would like to tell what to parse next by only looking at the next token in the input. Depending on the grammar this isn't always possible, and we might have to look two, three or more tokens ahead to decide what production we should use. The decision, however, must be unambiguous for this to work, hence the need sometimes to lookahead more than one token. We would also like to avoid backtracking, that is we'd rather not have to look at previous tokens in order to determine what to do next. Grammars that allow a parser to only look forward are called LL(k) grammars where k is the number of tokens it uses to lookahead and make decisions. The first L in LL refers to left-to-right parsing while the second L represents left-most derivations. There is also an alternative approach referred to as LR but these parsers are beyond the scope of this book.

In general, in order to ensure that a grammar is LL(k) we must:

- Remove common prefixes using left factoring.

- Remove any left recursion to avoid infinite loops.

- Remove any ambiguity in the grammar.

LL(k) Parser: This is a parser that needs to lookahead k token in order to parse a given language.

LL(k) Grammar: This is a grammar that can be parsed by a parser requiring only k lookahead tokens.

Definition:

A grammar is called LL(k) if sentences of the grammar can be parsed such that in each situation, where a choice must be made between several alternatives, the correct alternative can always be found by considering the next k symbols.

One of the nicer aspects of recursive descent combined with LL(1) is that the software is straightforward to write. We just create a procedure for each non-terminal, then implement the corresponding production rule. Since the grammar is LL(1), we only ever need to look one token ahead. This has made recursive descent popular with interpreter and compiler writers.

If one is confronted with an inability to select a way forward with one lookahead, it is usually best to modify the grammar if you're using recursive descent. If that is not possible then one needs to consider more advanced parsing approaches.

6.5.2   Left factoring

As mentioned before, ideally we'd prefer to look only one token ahead to determine what to do next. As a result, many practical grammars are designed to be LL(1). That is, it's only necessary to look forward one token in order to successfully parse the language. To give an example of a grammar that is not LL(1) consider the following:

```
stmt  = identifier '+' identifier | identifier '=' expression           (6.3)
```

Assume that the current token is `identifier`. With one token lookahead, it's not possible to decide from the token whether we should proceed with the first or second option in the production rule since both choices start with an `identifier`. To resolve this we would need to look two tokens ahead to check for the `'='` or `'+'`. This means we're dealing here with an LL(2) grammar. In general, most developers choose to design grammars that are LL(1) friendly. If a grammar is problematic in this way, the act of fixing it is called **left factoring**.

The general approach to removing common prefixes such as `identifier` in the previous example, is to apply the following rule. Given a production rule that has the common prefix α:

$$A = \alpha\beta_1 \mid \alpha\beta_2$$

Left factoring converts the production rule into two rules using the pattern:

$$A \quad = \alpha A'$$
$$A' = \beta_1 \mid \beta_2$$

For example in the grammar shown in (6.3) we can *factor* the grammar using the above rule. In this case:

α is identifer

β_1 is ('+' identifer)

β_2 is ('=' expression).

Applying the rules we obtain:

```
stmt = identifier A'
A' = '+' identifier | '=' expression
```

Notice that it is much easier to revolve. We apply rule stmt first and the choice is then between a plus or an equals symbol in the second production. In code, this would be written using two methods:

```
procedure stmt;
begin
   identifier();
   A1();
end;

procedure A1;
begin
  case sc.token of
     tPlus : begin sc.nextToken(); identifier(); end;
     tMult : begin sc.nextToken(); expression(); end;
  else
     raise ESyntaxError.Create ('Syntax error');
  end;
end;
```

In practice we'd probably combine the methods, effectively using the rule:

$$A = \alpha(\beta_1|\beta_2)$$

This also explains why it's called left factoring because we factor out the common prefix.

6.5.3 The dangling else

A very famous example of a syntax that cannot be parsed using LL(1) without careful thought given to the grammar is the dangling else. Consider the following two C code fragments that use if statements:

```
if (test_1)                     if (test_1)
   if (test_2)                     if (test_2)
      statement_1                     statement_1
   else                         else
      statement_2                     statement_2
```

To the human eye, it might appear that in the left case the else belongs to the second if statement and on the right, it appears that the else belongs to the first if statement. However, the lexical scanner will generate exactly the same tokens in each situation and the parser is unable to decide which case to use. There are various solutions to this problem. In the Rhodus language, we'll always have a terminating end after each block where the above example would be written as:

```
if test_1 then
   if test_2 then
      statement_1
   end
else
   statement_2
end
```

The order of execution of the statements after else is therefore clear. This is similar to the strategy that Perl uses. A more elaborate if\then\else construct for Rhodus would be:

```
if (x < y) then
   a = 5
else
   if (x > y) then
      a = 9
   else
      if (z < y) then
         a = 10
      else
         a = 1
      end
   end
end
```

Hopefully it's clear what else belongs to what if. The down-side is that we end up with a trail of terminating ends but I don't think this is a huge problem. One way around the trail of ends would be to implement elseif. We may revisit this in part 2.

6.5.4   Left recursion

The second problem that can prevent us from using recursive descent with LL(1) is left recursion. Consider the following production rule:

```
A = A B
```

If we write this as a procedure we get:

```
procedure A;
begin
  A();
  B();
end;
```

The problem here is that we've ended up in a recursive loop. That is production rule A calls itself, which calls itself and so on. Because we don't move to the next token, we're stuck with the same token over and over and there is no way to move forward. Such production rules are called **left recursive**; it's not possible to use recursive descent with such production rules. There are, however, standard techniques for removing left recursion from a grammar. Consider the left recursive grammar:

$$A = Ax \mid \beta$$

We can convert this rule to be non-left recursive by splitting the single rule into two rules, thus:

$$A = \beta A'$$
$$A' = xA' \mid \text{empty} \tag{6.4}$$

Notice that the second production, $A' = xA' \mid$ empty, is **right recursive** in A'. This isn't a problem because we have to get past x first which will move the token on one position so there is no chance of an infinite loop. Derivations will have the form $A' \Rightarrow x\ A' \Rightarrow xx$ $A' \Rightarrow xxx\ A' \Rightarrow xxxx\ A' \Rightarrow \dots$ until empty. Valid sentences will therefore be: x, xx, xxx, xxxx, xxxxx, etc. This is essentially repeating the production which means we can express the production using the iteration notation in EBNF. The equivalent in EBNF is:

$$A = \beta \{ x \}$$

Hence, one way to remove left-recursion is to use repetition. In the Rhodus interpreter we'll use this trick a number of times. For example assume we have the following left recursive production rule:

```
expression = expression '+' term | term
```

This rule cannot be parsed using a recursive descent parser. Instead we'll transform it using equation (6.4) to:

```
expression  = term expression1
expression1 = '+' term expression1 | empty
```

which in turn can be represented much more compactly using the repetition notation of EBNF:

```
expression = term { '+' term }
```

It also has the added advantage that the repetition form is easy to implement using a `while` loop. The reader should work their way through the grammar to show that the repetition form is equivalent.

6.5.5 Ambiguous grammars

It is possible to write a context-free grammar that is **ambiguous**. That is there is more than one way to apply the production rules. Note this is not the same as left factoring where we had identical choices between two or more production rules. A good example that illustrates the problem is a + b + c. Consider the grammar:

```
E = F | E + E
F = a | b | c
```

where E represents an expression. There are two ways to reach the a + b + c expression, and each has a different interpretation in terms of arithmetic. The two expression are either a + (b + c) or (a + b) + c, note the difference in bracketing. This stems from the way in which the production rules are applied. In this case, it doesn't really matter that we end up with two different interpretations because addition is not dependent on the order of execution. But if we were dealing with other operators, this would matter. For example the two expressions a - (b + c) or (a - b) + c will yield completely different answers. To convince you that the grammar is indeed ambiguous let's work through the left-derivations for the sentence a + b + c. Starting with E, the first derivation is as follows. Remember we will always be replacing the leftmost non-terminal:

$E \Rightarrow E + E \Rightarrow a + E \Rightarrow a + (E + E) \Rightarrow a + (b + E) \Rightarrow a + (b + c)$

The second way to do the left-derivation is:

$E \Rightarrow E + E \Rightarrow (E + E) + E \Rightarrow (a + E) + E \Rightarrow (a + b) + E \Rightarrow (a + b) + c$

Solving ambiguity turns out to be straightforward but we need to change the grammar. If we rewrite the previous grammar in the following way, the grammar is no longer ambiguous:

```
E = E + F | F
F = a | b | c
```

A left derivation yields:

$E \Rightarrow E + F \Rightarrow (E + F) + F \Rightarrow (F + F) + F) \Rightarrow (a + b) + c$

There is no other left derivation that works. The left derivation, (a + b) + c, is therefore unique and of course unambiguous. Note also that this left-derivation groups the terminals as we would normally do when computing the sum on paper, i.e., the first two terms first followed by the third term. Unfortunately, there is a problem; the grammar is left-recursive, so it can't be used in a recursive descent parser. However, all is not lost, we can transform the grammar into an iteration using the techniques discussed in the last section on left recursion. This yields:

```
E = F { * F }
F = a | b | c
```

We now have an unambiguous grammar that is not left-recursive and also importantly hasn't changed the meaning of the original grammar.

6.6 Designing a Simple Calculator

In this section, we will practice some of the theory by building a parser for a grammar that describes a simple calculator. The calculator will support addition, subtraction, multiplication, division, exponentiation, unary minus, and parentheses.

6.6.1 Initial syntax

We will make sure the grammar is LL(1) so that we can parse it using standard recursive descent with one token lookahead. We'll start by supporting addition, subtraction, multiplication, division, and parentheses. It turns out adding exponentiation, and the unary minus requires some thought. How about starting with a simple one-line production rule such as:

```
expression = expression '+' expression |  expression '-' expression
           |  expression '*' expression |  expression '/' expression
```

What could possibly go wrong? Actually quite a bit. Quite apart from the fact that the grammar is left recursive meaning the parser will go into an infinite loop, there is also ambiguity. When confronted with the expression 2 * 4 + 3, the production rule will compute the answer to be 18. As every middle schooler knows, the real answer should be 14. The problem with this production rule is that there is more than one way to parse an expression such as 2 + 4 * 3. Do we mean (2 + 4) * 3 or 2 + (4 * 3)? This is important because they give completely different answers. In normal arithmetic, we generally do multiplication before addition. That is multiplication has higher **precedence**.

Another problem is how would we handle an expression such as 1 - 2 - 3. Again there are two ways to interpret this, either (1-2)-3 or 1-(2-3) and they both give different answers. This is a problem of **associativity**. A standard way to deal with associativity is to state that expressions are read left to right so that something like a - b - c is interpreted as (a - b) - c. We say that the operator is **left associative**. In fact the operators +, -, * and / are all left associative, **except** for exponentiation, which is right-associative. This point will be revisited later on.

These kinds of issues lead to incorrect interpretation. They can be resolved however by careful design of the production rules. In particular, we can split the grammar into a number of production rules in order to enforce precedence so that some operators get resolved before others. In making such adjustments we arrive at a larger set of production rules as follows:

```
expression    = term { ('+' | '-' ) term }
term          = factor { ('*' | '/') factor }
factor        = '(' expression ')' | variable | number
```

If we start with expression we drop to term then to factor at which point we start winding out if we detect a variable or number. If not we recursively move back to expression and start again – assuming we detected a left parenthesis. Note that if we don't detect a left parenthesis, variable or number, then we have a syntax error to report.

Precedence is handled by moving the multiplication operators into their own production rule called term. Associatively is handled by making the production rules left recursive, but as we've seen recursive descent parsers can't handle left recursive grammars, they go into an infinite loop. So what do we do? We could use a right-recursive production rule, such as expression = term termOp expression | term but this will parse 1 - 2 - 3 as 1 - (2 - 3) which is not how we normally read such an expression.

To continue further, we need to introduce syntax trees.

6.6.2 Syntax trees

The tree data structure is a common way to organize data in a hierarchical fashion. Unlike a biological tree where the root is at the bottom, and the leaves towards the top, a tree data structure will often have the root at the top and the leaves near the bottom. Figure 6.3 shows a typical rendering of a tree. Every tree has a single root located at the top. From the root emanates one or more nodes. From these nodes, further nodes can emerge. If a node has no further nodes coming from it, that node is called a **leaf**. Sections of a tree are called **subtrees**.

Given that the grammar rules we've seen are hierarchical it shouldn't come as a surprise to learn that trees can be used to represent sentences form a language. Up to now we've written code to check whether a given sentence is consistent with the grammar. During the parsing we didn't record any information about what we parsed. Such information will be required when we eventually want to generate code to execute. The most convenient way to record the source code is to build what is called an **abstract syntax tree**, Figure 6.2. In

Part 1 we'll only give an brief introduction to abstract syntax trees and will reserve Part 2 for a model detailed discussion.

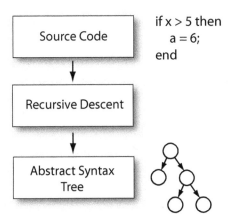

Figure 6.2 Source code to abstract syntax tree.

Not only can the tree record the structure of the source code but it can also indicate precedence. For example, consider the expression $3 \times 4 + 8$. We've drawn the expression as a tree shown in Figure 6.4. The figure shows two possible trees for this expression. The left-hand tree shows what it would look like if multiplication has precedence over addition while the right-hand one shows addition having precedence.

A syntax tree is another way to visualize a derivation. For example, if the production rule `term = number * number` is applied to the sentence `3 * 4`, then we'll obtain a tree with a node represented by the multiplication operator and the leaves by the numbers 3 and 4. For rules that include many sequential terms, such as `A = X1 X2 X3 X4`, the tree will have many leaves corresponding to `X1`, `X2`, etc. For grammars containing alternatives, the tree structure will depend on the input string. If the production rule is `factor = variable | number`, the tree will be a single leaf that represents either a variable or number depending on the input.

On a side note, a grammar is considered ambiguous if the same input string can be parsed into two different trees.

Many books will distinguish two types of tree in compiler and interpreter design, the parse tree, and the abstract syntax tree although in practice the separation isn't always seen in the software implementation. By a parse tree we mean a tree that is a literal representation of the syntax, this will include things such parentheses, semicolons, and the names of the non-terminals in the nodes. Much of this, however, can be removed. For example, precedence is already implicitly given by the structure of the tree so we don't need to record the parentheses. In addition, in an abstract syntax tree, the non-terminals are replaced with the operators. This results in a more compact and more manageable tree. In the software we'll write, we will generate the abstract syntax tree directly as we parse the source code.

When constructing a tree using recursive descent, we will use the following rules:

1. We only create a subtree from the production rule once we have identified the components in the production rule. This means drilling down into the grammar, identifying the terminal symbols and unwinding back to the production rule, at which point we construct the corresponding subtree. For example if the production rule were A op B, where op is an operator, we would create a subtree with a node that represents op and two leaves A and B.

2. Once we've constructed the subtree, we return it to the caller so that the caller can continue building its subtree.

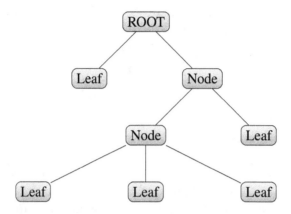

Figure 6.3 Tree structure showing, root, nodes, and leaves.

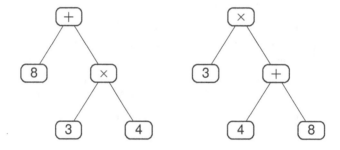

Figure 6.4 Two different ways to represent $3 \times 4 + 8$ using a tree structure. The left-hand true assumes multiplication has precedence, the right-hand one assumes addition has precedence.

For rules such as `term { * term }` that have repetition, we generate a subtree each time a repetition is identified. To make this clearer, consider the following example 1 - 2 - 3. The production rules we'll use are:

```
E = term { '-' term }
term = number
```

The derivation based on 1-2-3 is:

```
E ⇒ term {'-' term} ⇒ 1 {'-' term} ⇒ 1 {'-' 2}
   ⇒ (1 - 2) {'-' term} ⇒ (1 - 2) {'-' 3} ⇒ (1 - 2) - 3
```

Note that the ordering of the terms means that the expression is represented in the way we'd expect if evaluating it by pen and paper, that is (1-2) followed by -3. Knowing the derivation, we can create a tree (Figure 6.5).

We match the first term which generates a leaf for the number 1. If we detect a minus symbol, we match the second `term` which generates a leaf for the number 2. We then create a subtree between the two leaves with the minus symbol as the root node. We'll call this subtree T_1 (Figure 6.5). However, the production rule has a repetition, so we continue looking for any further minus symbols. We find another, - 3. We create a new subtree, where the node is the minus symbol and the two leaves are the previous subtree T_1 and the number 3. As a result, we obtain the tree structure shown in Figure 6.5. This approach ensures we achieve left associativity where we read the expression left to right. This avoids the situation 1-(2-3). The production method will then return T_2 to the caller.

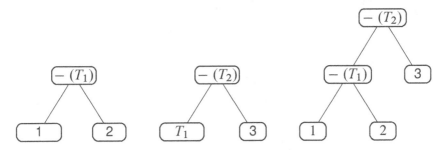

Figure 6.5 Growing tree from left to right as we parse 1 - 2 - 3.

To summarize, the purpose of syntax analysis two fold:

1. Make sure the source code is consistent with the language grammar.

2. Convert the source code into a more convenient representation such as an abstract syntax tree.

We'll have a lot more to say about abstract syntax tree in Part 2 of the series.

6.6.3 Grammar for a simple calculator

Let us now write down the grammar for the calculator. We've also added support for assignments and printing out expressions. This yields the following grammar for the initial iteration of the calculator:

```
program        = assignment | outputStatement
```

```
assignment        = variable '=' expression
outputStatement   = print expression
expression        = term { ('+' | '-') term }
term              = factor { ('*' | '/') factor }
factor            = '(' expression ')' | number | variable
```

You might notice that there is recursion in the grammar. For example, an expression is made up of `terms` which in turn is made up of factors which in turn can be made of more expressions. The following expressions are legitimate sentences based on this grammar:

```
print 1 + 2
a = 5.4/603
b = 3.0*5 - 64.3*(3+6)
```

6.7 Implementing the Calculator

Let's start writing some code. The first thing to do is create a new project which we will call `REPL_Project_SyntaxConsole`. We'll add the unit `uScanner.pas` to the project as well as a new unit called `uSyntaxAnalysis.pas`. `uScanner.pas` will be the same unit from Chapter 3. I would not make a copy of `uScanner.pas` but instead refer to the unit from the lexical analysis project. This is to avoid any chance of ending up with two `uScanner.pas` files that have diverged.

`uSyntaxAnalysis.pas` will contain a new class called `TSyntaxAnalysis`. We will need to include a constructor which will take a `TScanner` object reference as an argument so that the syntax class has access to the lexical analyzer. For every non-terminal symbol in the grammar, we must create a method. Only one of these methods needs to be public; this will be the `program` production rule. All the other production rule methods can be private. We'll also add a variable to store the `TScanner` instance called `sc`. The highest non-terminal in the grammar is `program`, we'll call it `myProgram` because `program` is a reserved word in Object Pascal.

The skeleton for this code is shown below:

```
unit uSyntaxAnalysis;

interface

Uses SysUtils, uScanner;

type
   TSyntaxAnalysis = class (TObject)
       private
          sc : TScanner;
          procedure factor;
```

```
         procedure term;
         procedure expression;
         procedure assignment;
         procedure outputStatement;
      public
         procedure myProgram;
         constructor Create (sc : TScanner);
   end;

implementation

constructor TSyntaxAnalysis.Create (sc : TScanner);
begin
end;

procedure TSyntaxAnalysis.expression;
begin
end;

procedure TSyntaxAnalysis.factor;
begin
end;

procedure TSyntaxAnalysis.term;
begin
end;

procedure TSyntaxAnalysis.assignment;
begin
end;

procedure TSyntaxAnalysis.outputStatement;
begin
end;

procedure TSyntaxAnalysis.myProgram;
begin
end;

end.
```

We now need to fill out each of the methods. The constructor is easy; we just copy over the TScanner object reference to our private variable sc as shown below:

```
constructor TSyntaxAnalysis.Create (sc : TScanner);
begin
  inherited Create;
  self.sc := sc;
end;
```

The production rule for factor is:

```
factor = '(' expression ')' | number | variable
```

This is a series of alternatives which we can easily implement using a case statement as follows:

```
procedure TSyntaxAnalysis.factor;
begin
  case sc.token of
    tInteger       : begin sc.nextToken; end;
    tFloat         : begin sc.nextToken; end;
    tIdentifier    : begin sc.nextToken; end;
    tLeftParenthesis :
        begin
        sc.nextToken;
        expression;
        expect (tRightParenthesis);
        end;
  else
     raise ESyntaxError.Create('expecting identifier, scalar or left parentheses');
  end;
end;
```

We'll look for both integers and floating point numbers. We have to remember to retrieve the next token whenever we recognize a terminal symbol. The case statement for the left parenthesis calls expression after which it expects a right parenthesis. Remember that `expect` will call `nextToken` for us. If the method doesn't find any of the expected tokens, it raises an exception.

At this point in time, we're just parsing the code and nothing else. Something that just parsers code and nothing else is often called a **recognizer**.

The two methods `term` and `expression` are very similar except one focuses on addition type operators and the other on multiplication type operators. In both cases we have to take into account the possible repetition of the operators to deal with situations like: a + b + c + ... or a * b * c * .... Recall that the production rules were:

```
expression = term { ('+' | '-') term }
term       = factor { ('*' | '/') factor }
```

The code is easily written based on this knowledge:

```
procedure TSyntaxAnalysis.term;
begin
  factor;
  while sc.token in [tMult, tDivide] do
    begin
    sc.nextToken;
    factor;
    end;
end;
```

```
procedure TSyntaxAnalysis.expression;
begin
  term;
  while sc.token in [tPlus, tMinus] do
    begin
    sc.nextToken;
    term;
    end;
end;
```

Note again that each time we recognize a terminal we call `nextToken`. The next method to deal with is `outputStatement`. This is quite easy to handle, we get the next token then call the `expression` production method:

```
procedure TSyntaxAnalysis.outputStatement;
begin
  sc.nextToken;
  expression;
end;
```

You may question why we're calling `nextToken` at the start of the method? To be consistent, we should have called `nextToken` the minute we identified the `print` token. However, I wanted to keep the code that identifies `print` relatively clean so I opted to move `nextToken` to the production rule method itself. This may not be agreeable to everyone, but it's easy to change of course.

The last method in the syntax unit will be `assignment` which has the production rule: `assignment = variable '=' expression`. This is very straightforward though we'll see some complications when we come to extend the calculator in Chapter 8:

```
procedure TSyntaxAnalysis.assignment;
begin
  expect (tIdentifier);
  expect (tEquals);
  expression;
end;
```

Finally, we deal with the top level production rule which is:

`program = assignment | outputStatement`

As mentioned before we can't use `program` as the name for the method because `program` is a reserved word in Object Pascal. So we'll use `myProgram` instead. The code for `myProgram` is shown below:

```
procedure TSyntaxAnalysis.myProgram;
begin
  sc.nextToken;
```

```
  case sc.token of
     tIdentifier : assignment;
     tPrint      : outputStatement
  else
     raise ESyntaxError.Create('expecting assignment or print statement');
end;
```

To use the new syntax class, we need to modify the REPL. Specifically, we remove the section from scanString and substitute in the following code.

```
if sourceCode <> '' then
  begin
  sc.scanString(sourceCode);
  try
    sy.myProgram;
  except
    on e:ESyntaxError do
      writeln ('Error: ' + e.Message);
  end;
```

We'll also add sy := TSyntaxAnalysis.Create (sc) to instantiate the syntax analysis class into a variable sy. Recall that the constructor takes an instance of TScanner. We can add this constructor to the line just after we create the TScanner instance. I also removed the initial sc.nextoken call and moved it into myProgram. The new REPL code is shown below. One point of note is how the TScanner and TSyntaxAnalysis objects are created and freed. The correct approach is to have two nested try/finally blocks, one for TScanner and the second for TSyntaxAnalysis. This arrangement is shown below:

```
begin
  sc := TScanner.Create;
  try
    sy := TSyntaxAnalysis.Create (sc);
    try
      displayWelcome;
      while True do
        begin
        displayPrompt;
        readln (sourceCode);
        if sourceCode = 'quit' then
          break;

        if sourceCode <> '' then
          begin
          sc.scanString(sourceCode);
          try
            sy.myProgram;
          except
            on e:exception do
              writeln ('Error: ' + e.Message);
```

```
            end;
          end;
        end;
     writeln ('Press any key to exit');
     readln;
    finally
      sy.Free;
    end;
  finally
    sc.Free;
  end;
end.
```

The alternative, but **incorrect** approach, is to use the following:

```
// Don't do it this way
begin
  sc := TScanner.Create;
  sy := TSyntaxAnalysis.Create (sc);
  try
     ... run parser
  finally
    sc.Free; st.Free;
  end;
end.
```

In this case, we have a single `try/finally` that will free both objects. What can happen here (though unlikely), is that the constructor for `TSyntaxAnalysis` could fail and raise an exception. This will cause a memory leak in `sc` because the `finally` section won't be called leaving `sc` unfreed.

We're now ready to run our new parser. The following is a sample of some of the output we can get. I've included some bad syntax to illustrate the syntax errors that we catch. The final test shows that we will still catch scanner exceptions, in this case, an integer overflow.

```
Welcome to Rhodus Syntax Analysis Console, Version 1.0
Data and Time: 12/1/2018, 3:52:01 PM
Type quit to exit
>> a = 2
>> a =
Error: expecting identifier, scalar or left parentheses
>> a = 2 + 5
>> 2
Error: expecting assignment or print statement
>> print 2
>> print 3/
Error: expecting identifier, scalar or left parentheses
>> print 2*3.1415*r*r + alpha/beta - 1
>>
>> print 12345678901234567
```

```
Error: integer overflow, constant value too large to read
>>
```

At the moment the program just does syntax checking so don't expect a `print` 2+3 statement to actually print 5 to the console. We'll make the calculator to do that next.

6.7.1   Make the calculator calculate

Although it's not quite the direction we're going to ultimately take with the interpreter, let's show how we can make the calculator calculate with just a few changes. This subproject will also give us an opportunity to revisit operator precedence. We won't support `assignments` or variable names in this version of the calculator. We'll also add the restriction that expressions can only be composed of literal numbers.

For this subproject, we'll make a completely new group called `CalculatorGroup` and put the calculator project in that. We'll call this project `CalculatorProject`. We'll need `uScanner.pas` and `uSyntaxAnalysis.pas`. This time I would make copies of these files for the new project. One reason is that we're going to remove some code from `uSyntax-Analysis.pas`. In particular we'll remove `assignment`, `myProgram` and `outputExpression`. We'll also move `expression` to the public interface. The methods that are left, `term`, `factor` and `expression` are going to be turned into functions that return a double. Although this is a dead-end subproject in the sense it won't evolve much further, it will serve a useful a purpose in explaining more about precedence and enable us to more thoroughly test the expression grammar. In Part 2 we'll return to the previous project and use that to continue building the interpreter.

The new syntax class for the calculator will look like:

```
TSyntaxAnalysis = class (TObject)
   private
     sc : TScanner;
     procedure expect (expectedToken : TTokenCode);
     function factor : double;
     function term : double;
   public
     function    expression : double;
     constructor Create (sc : TScanner);
   end;
```

How do we use what we learned about syntax trees to make the calculator compute? Recall that when constructing a particular production rule, the idea is to resolve the production rule, generate the resulting subtree and return the subtree to the caller. For the calculator, instead of building a tree, we'll compute the result. This means instead of returning a subtree to the caller we return a double value. This explains why we modified the signature of the production methods to return a double.

With this in mind, we need to modify the code in each of the production rule methods. This time, not only do they check that the tokens match the expected syntax but they will carry out the calculations implied in the production rule. In the case of factor it would normally return a reference to a leaf, but in the calculator, it will return the value of the leaf. As a result, the `factor` method will change to:

```
function TSyntaxAnalysis.factor : double;
begin
  case sc.token of
    tInteger      : begin sc.nextToken; result := sc.tokenInteger; end;
    tFloat        : begin sc.nextToken; result := sc.tokenFloat; end;
    tLeftParenthesis :
        begin
        sc.nextToken;
        result := expression;
        expect (tRightParenthesis);
        end;
  else
    raise ESyntaxError.Create('expecting scalar or left parentheses');
  end;
end;
```

When we find an integer or double token we return the corresponding value of the token. Recall that the token is stored in a record of type `TTokenElement`. The record allows us to store the properties of the token, for example, the numeric and string values. Whenever we retrieve a `tInteger` or `tFloat` token we'll also be able to get the actual value. Hence when `factor` detects an integer value it will return the value of the integer using `sc.tokenInteger`. The same goes for the floating point token, but this time it returns `sc.tokenFloat`. If we detect parentheses, we call expression and expression will return a numeric value which we will then return from `factor`. You can probably see where this is going.

Consider `term` which deals with multiplication like operators. This method would normally return a subtree corresponding to a node that represents the operator and two leaves corresponding to the two calls to factor. Instead of returning a subtree we will return the result of the calculation. This method is shown below:

```
function TSyntaxAnalysis.term : double;
begin
  result := factor;
  while sc.token in [tMult, tDivide] do
      begin
      if sc.token = tMult then
        begin
        sc.nextToken;
        result := result * factor;
        end
      else
        begin
```

```
        sc.nextToken;
        result := result / factor;
        end;
    end;
end;
```

We first capture the return value from the call to factor. If we detect a multiplication or division, we need to apply the corresponding operation to the two factors we have at hand. Note that we keep updating the `result` variable in the while loop if there are multiple operators such as a * b * c * ... The same logic is used for `expression` which deals with the addition like operators, as shown below:

```
function TSyntaxAnalysis.expression : double;
begin
  result := term;
  while sc.token in [tPlus, tMinus] do
    begin
    if sc.token = tPlus then
        begin
        sc.nextToken;
        result := result + factor;
        end
    else
        begin
        sc.nextToken;
        result := result - term;
        end;
    end;
end;
```

`expression` has the same basic structure as `term`.

The other change we have to make is to the REPL. We'll use exactly the same REPL code but instead of calling `sy.myProgram` we'll now call `sy.expression`. Since `expression` returns a double result, we'll also write it out as shown below:

```
sc.nextToken;
writeln (sy.expression:12:8);
```

We have to call `sc.nextToken` because this was originally inside `myProgram`. I changed the welcome message as well. And that's it. Let's run this code to see what it does. The console session below shows some typical results when we run the calculator:

```
Welcome to the simple calculator, Version 1.0
Data and Time: 12/3/2018, 2:59:52 PM
Only supports expressions, no assignment of variable names, e.g
2+3,  4/(6-7),  4*3+8E-4*50, 2^3, ---4
Type quit to exit
>> 2+3
```

```
  5.0000
>> 2-3
 -1.0000
>> 2*3
  6.0000
>> 2/3
  0.6667
>> 1+2+3+4
 10.0000
>> 1-2-3
 -4.0000
>> 1-(2-3)
  2.0000
>> (1-2)-3
 -4.0000
>> 1/0
Error: Floating point division by zero
>> (3+6)*3 - 6/7 + 0
 26.1429
>> quit
Press any key to exit
```

You might want to imagine what's going on in the code as it parses an expression. It works its way to the leaves of the syntax tree and then climbs back out calculating the subtrees in turn until its all the way out. Once it reaches the root, it has the final result.

A couple of things are worth pointing out in the output from the above session. Associatively works, that is 1-2-3 is calculated correctly, and we can also override the order using parentheses. One thing we got for free was the divide by zero exception which was caught. However, we might deal with divide by zero explicitly in future rather than let the runtime system handle it.

Something else worth trying is how the calculator deals with overflows. We can't test for integer overflows because all the calculations in the code are done using floating point. In any case, integer overflow checking is disabled by default in the Delphi compiler, and we haven't turned it on in the code. We can try to induce a floating overflow response by calculating, for example, 1E200*1E200 as shown below:

```
>> 1E200*1E200
Error: Floating point overflow
>>
```

6.7.2 Adding exponentiation and the unary minus

There are a number of major items missing from our calculator. A test that highlights one of the most glaring omissions can be seen in the following session:

```
Welcome to the simple calculator, Version 1.0
Data and Time: 12/3/2018, 3:20:30 PM
Type quit to exit
>> -3
Error: expecting scalar or left parentheses
>> +3
Error: expecting scalar or left parentheses
>>
```

The calculator can't handle the unary minus or plus. For example, the number -3 makes no sense to it. A unary operation is one that only operates on one mathematical object. This is in contrast to binary operations such as summation that require two mathematical objects. The lack of unary support means we can't deal with expressions such as 2-(-3), even expressions such as +5 fail. To handle unary operators we need to think first about operator precedence. Let's look at some expressions that use the unary minus. The first one is:

-2+4

We expect this to evaluate to +2 because we consider the minus in front of -2 to be more important than the summation. In other words, the unary minus has higher precedence than the binary operator plus. If it didn't we'd expect the answer -6 which isn't what we'd expect. This also applies to an expression such as:

-2-4

this will evaluate to -6 which is expected if the unary minus if computed first. The alternative is that it evaluates to 2, i.e. 2-4 then negate. This doesn't seem right based on how we normally deal with such arithmetic. It would make sense if we wrote it as -(2-4). What about expressions such as:

2--3 or 2---3

These aren't typos. Python, R, and Julia and the web 2.0 calculator at https://web2.0calc.com/ for example will accept this syntax. Just to be clear, 2--3 will evaluate to 5 and 2---3 will evaluate to -1. However many online calculators won't even let you type multiple minuses in a row. Both Octave and Javascript will report a syntax error when confronted with 2---3. Those systems that can't evaluate such expressions will correctly evaluate them if they a bracketed, such as 2-(-2) or 2-(-(-2)). Those languages that do accept such expressions will generate the expected results, thus 2--2 will resolve to 4 and 2---2 will resolve to zero in Python.

Something else we don't support is exponentiation which we'd like to do in Rhodus. This will include expressions such as 2^3 or 2^3^4. Things get worse when we mix in unary operators. Including unary operators and exponentiation appears to be a precarious place for language designers. There is some variability in how these operators are treated with Excel probably being the most famous at generating "unconventional results". For example -2^2 in Excel is 4 when it should, by other standards be -4. Interestingly standard hand-

Operator	Precedence
not, ()	Boolean **not**, parentheses
^	Exponentiation
$+x$, $-x$	Unary operators
*, /, **div, mod, and**	Multiplication, division, integer division, modulus, Boolean **and**
+, -, **or, xor**	Addition, subtraction, Boolean **or** and **xor**
<, <=, >, >=, !=,==	Comparisons

Table 6.3 Order of Presentence for Operators, with Highest at the Top. Modeled after Pascal Precedence.

held calculators will also compute 4 whereas more sophisticated calculators such as the HP Prime will compute -4.

However this isn't just a matter of sign changes, consider this calculation: 8^(-1^(-8^7)). I am sure most mathematicians and programming languages (except Javascript treats it as invalid syntax) would evaluate this expression to 1/8 but Excel will evaluate it to 8. Standard hand-held calculators will also output 8, whereas the HP Prime will output 1/8.

How do we deal with expressions such as:

-3^2

In this case, we expect the answer to be -9. If you try this in Python (type -3**2) or Julia (-3^2) you'll get -9. This means that exponentiation, '^', has **higher** precedence than the unary minus. The alternative is +9 that originates from (-3)^2 where the unary minus has higher precedence, however, this is not what we want. We will ensure that we follow standard expectations such that the unary minus has lower priority than exponentiation.

If we were to form a table of operator precedence, it would look like the one shown in Table 6.3. This has been modelled after the Pascal precedence list where exponentiation has been added. The higher precedence of exponentiation means it will be carried out before applying a unary minus or plus.

We still have to deal with something like 2--3 which equals 5. There is one trick we can do with respect to exponentiation. Because it's right-associative we can actually combine the unary minus support in with the exponentiation. As a reminder, right-association means that 2^3^4 evaluates in the order 2^(3^4) and not (2^3)^4. First let's update the EBNF:

```
factor      = '(' expression ')' | number
power       = { '+' | '-' } factor [ '^' power]
term        = power { ('*' | '/') power }
expression  = term { ('+' | '-') term }
```

We've introduced a new production with a non-terminal called power. We've combined the unary minus and exponentiation into one production rule. We can do this because exponentiation is right-associative so this preserved the requirement that the unary minus is computed after exponentiation. Note that the plus and minus symbols in power are also repeatable. This helps us deal with expressions such as --2 or --2^4. If there is no exponentiation operator, power goes directly to factor. The final thing to note is that the production rule is recursive in power. This deals with situations such as 2^3^4. We couldn't use a repeated option here such as { ^ power } because it still needs to watch for unary operators and the best way to do that is to call itself. It is also right-associative so it won't go into an infinite loop.

To give an example of a more complicated expression, we can try this one:

2*-(--1+2)^-(2+5*--(2+4))

not that any sane person would write such an expression. It shows however that the production rules can deal with complex situations.

Now back to the code to implement the modifications we made to the production rules. The one new method we have to add is the power production rule which is given below:

```
function TSyntaxAnalysis.power : double;
var sign : integer;
begin
  sign := 1;
  while (sc.token = tMinus) or (sc.token = tPlus) do
    begin
    if sc.token = tMinus then
        sign := -1*sign;
    sc.nextToken;
    end;

  result := factor;
  if sc.token = tPower then
    begin
    sc.nextToken;
    result := Math.Power (result, power);
    end;
  result := sign*result;
end;
```

There are a couple of things worth pointing out. In the first half of the method, we collect any unary operators and update the sign variable to take them into account. For example -- sets sign to +1 while --- sets sign to -1. A plus operator doesn't result in any sign change. To ensure that the exponentiation is right-associative we only multiply the sign value into the result **after** we've dealt with the exponentiation.

We also have to remember to call power rather than factor in term in line 9 and 14 in the following code:

```
1  function TSyntaxAnalysis.term : double;
2  begin
```

```
3    result := power;
4    while sc.token in [tMult, tDivide] do
5       begin
6       if sc.token = tMult then
7          begin
8          sc.nextToken;
9          result := result * power
10         end
11      else
12         begin
13         sc.nextToken;
14         result := result / power;
15         end;
16      end;
17   end;
```

With these changes a typical output from the new version is shown below:

```
Welcome to the simple calculator, Version 1.0
Data and Time: 12/5/2018, 12:19:10 PM
Type quit to exit
>> -3
 -3.00000000
>> ---3
 -3.00000000
>> -2+4
  2.00000000
>> 2^3^2
512.00000000
>> -2^3
 -8.00000000
>>   2---3^4
-79.00000000
>> 8^(-1^(-8^7))
  0.12500000
>> 2*--(----1+2)^-(2+5*---(2+4))
45753584909922.00000000
>>
```

This code will require a fair amount of testing, and we'll reserve that for the next Chapter.

6.7.3   Boolean operators and comparisons

The C related languages such as C, C++, etc. tend to put the Boolean operators near the bottom of the precedence table, certainly below the comparison operators. In Pascal-like languages, such as Modula-2 and Oberon-2, the Boolean operators are associated with arithmetic operators. This is reasonable if you consider the operation AND is in some sense a multiplication and the OR is a form of addition. We will deal with Boolean operators in Chapter 9.

6.7.4 Error handling

One thing we've not really discussed is using a more sophisticated error handling approach. Currently, the moment we detect an error we exit immediately. Sometimes this is called the catastrophic approach to error handling. One could imagine however that if the error were localized (such as an overflow error), we could issue the error message and then continue parsing as if nothing had happened. If there is an error, we won't be able to run the code, but the user can get a list of errors in the source code. We'll leave more sophisticated error handling to Part 2 of the series where we'll introduce FIRST and FOLLOW sets.

6.8 Specification for Version 1 of Rhodus

Before we leave this chapter let's define the syntax for version one of Rhodus using EBNF. In the following keywords are shown in all capitals.

Full syntax grammar for version one of Rhodus:

```
mainProgram       = statementList [ ';' ] endOfStream
statementList     = statement { ; statement }
statement         = assignment | forStatement | ifStatement
                        | whileStatement | repeatStatement
                        | returnStatment | breakStatement
                        | function | endOfStream
variable          = simpleVariable | indexVariable
list              = '{' [ expressionList ] '}'
simpleVariable    = identifier
indexVariable     = identifier '[' expressionList ']'
expressionList    = expression { ',' expression }
assignment        = variable '=' expression
function          = FUNCTION identifier '(' [ argumentList ] ')' functionBody
functionBody      = statementList END
argumentList      = argument { ',' argument }
argument          = identifier | REF variable
returnStatement   = RETURN expression
breakStatement    = BREAK
expression        = simpleExpression | simpleExpression relationalOp simpleExpression
simpleExpression  = term { addingOp term }
term              = factor { multiplyOp factor }
power             = { '+' | '-'} factor [ '^' power ]
factor            = '(' expression ')' | variable | number | string |
                        NOT factor | list | functionCall
functionCall      = identifier '(' [ expressionList ] ')'
addingOp          = '+' | '-' | OR | XOR
multiplyOp        = '*' | '/' | AND | MOD | DIV
```

```
relationalOp        = '==' | '!=' | '<' | '<=' | '>=' | '>'
whileStatement      = WHILE expression DO statementList END
repeatStatement     = REPEAT statementList UNTIL expression
forStatement        = FOR identifier = forList DO statementList END
forList             = value TO value | value DOWNTO value
ifStatement         = IF expression THEN statementList ifEnd
ifEnd               = END | ELSE statementList END
```

6.9   Online Resources

1. A Stanford group has developed a CFG Developer tool. This allows one to enter a grammar and the tool will create a derivation for a user-specified input string.

https://web.stanford.edu/class/archive/cs/cs103/cs103.1156/tools/cfg/

2. Another but perhaps more comprehensive CFG tool by 'Anton'. This supports an iteration syntax and also has the capacity to draw the parse trees.

https://planetcalc.com/5600/

6.10   Glossary

This is an informal glossary of common terms.

Terminals

A terminal is a symbol of a language that cannot be broken down any simpler. For example '+'

Non-Terminals

A non-terminal is a higher level construct in the language, for example, a = 2 represents a non-terminal called an assignment.

Production Rule

A production rule is a rule that states how a non-terminal can be replaced by other terminals or non-terminals in the language.

Start symbol

The start symbol is the highest order construct in the language and from which all sentences in the language can be derived.

Context-free Grammar

A context-free grammar has the following properties and components:

1) A set of terminal symbols;
2) A set of non-terminal symbols;
3) A set of production rules where the left-hand side is a single non-terminal and the right-

hand side one or more terminals and non-terminals;

4) A start symbol.

Associativity

The interpretation of a sequence of operations which involve the operators of the same precedence, e.g., a - b - c is called associativity. The order can be left or right associative.

Precedence

Precedence refers to the order of the operations when evaluating a mathematical expression. For example, multiplication should come before addition.

Grammar

A grammar is a set of production rules that describe syntactically valid sentences in a given language.

LL(k)

A grammar is called LL(k) if sentences of the grammar can be parsed such that in each situation where a choice must be made between several alternatives, the correct alternative can always be found by considering the net k symbols.

Further Reading

There is a lot of material online that describes parsing and grammars. Wikipedia, of course, has much but it tends to be fairly academic. There are also a number of books and online resources that describe compiler tools such as yacc and ANTLR. A very readable introduction to yacc is given by Tom Niemann `https://www.epaperpress.com/lexandyacc/`. The HOC calculator also provides a nice application of yacc. Note that Bison is the GNU equivalent of yacc.

1. Johnson, Stephen C. (1975) Yacc: Yet Another Compiler Compiler. Computing Science Technical Report No. 32, Bell Laboratories, Murray Hill, New Jersey.

7

Testing the Calculator

7.1 Testing the Calculator

In the last chapter, we built a simple calculator that could do addition, subtraction, multiplication, division, unary minus, exponentiation, and parentheses. Why bother to build this when we are going to build a virtual machine that can execute bytecode? The calculator project is, in fact, an excellent platform to test whether our calculator grammar is correct. There were some subtleties in the expression parser, especially when it dealt with exponentiation and the unary minus. In truth, I went through a number of iterations before I got a working grammar. It is interesting to note that combining exponentiation and the unary minus is not often mentioned either in compiler books or the internet. This is likely because languages such as C/C++ or Java don't have explicit support for exponentiation.[1]

Although the calculator received some testing, it wasn't extensive. I'm reasonably confident that the expression grammar is correct, however, it needs a thorough test to make sure nothing is wrong. As before, we'll set up a parallel project in the calculator group to carry out the testing. We won't actually be doing unit testing, but rather system testing, that is, expected behavior based on specific inputs.[2]

---

[1]In the end, I received some help from 'rici' on StackOverflow, and I am indebted to him/her for resolving several issues.

[2]The code for this chapter can be found in GitHub in the Calculator_Chapr6 folder.

7.2   Setting up and Using DUnitX

First, create a new DUnitX project within the existing calculator project. Do this by right-clicking over the group and selecting a new project, find the DUnitX project, and select. Fill in the entries in the wizard as we did before. I named the test fixture to `TCalculatorTest`, and I named the project to `ProjectUnitCalculatorTest`. I brought in `uScanner.pas` and `uSyntaxAnalysis.pas` into the project. I renamed the unit that contains the test to `uCalculatorUnitTest.pas`. With that done I added the tests. I also added two tests that raised exceptions: divide by zero and unbalanced parentheses. I added a few odd looking expressions such as 2**3, 2^^4 and 2-3- to make sure the parser caught some of these errors. In fact, these tests uncovered an error in my exception handling where I was raising `Exception` instead of `ESyntaxException`. I also added 2//4. Note that this contains a comment, and the calculator will return 2, which it does correctly. The good news is that no errors were reported except for the incorrect exception type.

```
[Test]
[TestCase('Test1','1,1')]
[TestCase('Test2','+1,1')]
[TestCase('Test3','-1,-1')]
[TestCase('Test4','-2,-2')]
[TestCase('Test5','+123,123')]
[TestCase('Test6','2+3,5')]
[TestCase('Test7','2-3,-1')]
[TestCase('Test8','2*3,6')]
[TestCase('Test9','6/2,3')]
[TestCase('Test10','2.4+2.1,4.5')]
[TestCase('Test11','2.4-2.2,0.2')]
[TestCase('Test12','2.4*2.2,5.28')]
[TestCase('Test13','6.5/2.4,2.708333333')]
[TestCase('Test14','2*3+4,10')]
[TestCase('Test15','2+3*4,14')]
[TestCase('Test16','1 + 2 - 3 - 5 - 1 + 0 - 4 + 2,-8')]
[TestCase('Test17','2*1*3*5*3*2,180')]
[TestCase('Test18','(2),2')]
[TestCase('Test19','(2+4),6')]
[TestCase('Test20','(2+3)*4,20')]
[TestCase('Test21','(((2))),2')]
[TestCase('Test22','((2)+4)*((5)),30')]
[TestCase('Test23','-2+24,22')]
[TestCase('Test24','3-(-5),8')]
[TestCase('Test25','+5-(+7),-2')]
[TestCase('Test26','-5+(-7),-12')]
[TestCase('Test27','-2*(3-5)+7,11')]
[TestCase('Test28','5.5*(2-3 + (5.3-7.89)/2)/2,-6.31125')]
[TestCase('Test29','2-(32-4)/(23+(4)/(5))-(2-4)*(4+6-98.2)+4,-171.5764705882352')]
[TestCase('Test31','2^3,8')]
[TestCase('Test31','8^(-1^(-8^7)),0.125')]
[TestCase('Test32','2^(-3),0.125')]
```

```
[TestCase('Test33','2^0.7,1.624505')]
[TestCase('Test34','4^3^2,262144')]
[TestCase('Test35','(4^3)^2,4096')]
[TestCase('Test36','0.9^0.8^0.7^0.6^0.5,0.9148883')]
[TestCase('Test37','-2^3,-8')]
[TestCase('Test38','2/3/4,0.166666666')]
[TestCase('Test39','2--3,5')]
[TestCase('Test40','2---3,-1')]
[TestCase('Test41','2---3^4,-79')]
[TestCase('Test42','2*-(1+2)^-(2+5*-(2+4)),-4.5753584909922e+13')]
[TestCase('Test43','2//4,2')]
procedure TestCalculator(const sourceCode : string; const expectedResult : double);
[Test]
procedure TestDivideByZero; // 1/0
[Test]
procedure TestUnbalancedParentheses; // (0
[Test]
procedure Test_two_stars; // 2**3
[Test]
procedure Test_two_hats; // 2^^3
[Test]
procedure Test_two_3_; // 2-3-
```

8

Adding Assignments

8.1   One Last Thing for the Calculator

Previously we built a simple calculator that could do addition, subtraction, multiplication, division, unary minus, exponentiation, and parentheses. Let's do one last thing to the calculator, add assignments.[1] Adding assignments introduces two new ideas, the need for a symbol table and a grammatical problem with handling assignments. First, let's describe what kind of behavior we'd like to see in the calculator. If the user types in an assignment such as:

```
a = 2
```

we expect a symbol called a to be assigned a value 2. Such symbols will be stored in a symbol table. If the symbol doesn't exist, it will be created so that the assignment can proceed. If the symbol does exist, the value currently assigned to the symbol will be overwritten by the new value in the assignment. We will also allow symbols to appear on the right-hand side, such as:

```
a = b + 2
```

This will require us to change the `factor` method. Another thing we'll let a user do is enter the symbol name or a full expression at the console. For example:

```
a
a+2
```

[1]The code for this chapter can be found in GitHub in the Calculator_Chapr8 folder.

In this case, we expect the interpreter to evaluate a or a+2 and return the result to the console for display. You may have already realized there is a problem. Here is the simplified grammar in EBNF that supports this scenario:

```
assignment = variable '=' expression
expression = variable
```

I've made the example grammar purposefully simple so that `expression` is just a `variable` (obviously in the real grammar specification it would describe a full expression). What it shows is that it's not possible to parse this grammar with only a single lookahead, because it's not possible to distinguish between an `assignment` and a `variable`. The only way to know is to look ahead one more token to see if there is a `'='` symbol after the first token. For example, look at the following two inputs:

```
a = 2
a
```

This is therefore not a LL(1) grammar but more like a LL(2). How do we get around this problem? There are several options that can be used. In the C language assignment is treated as an arithmetic operator. In fact, assignments in C can return values. For example, consider this legal C fragment:

```
if ((result = getValue()) == -1) etc
```

In C, an assignment such as a = b will return a. This solution is not something I want to use.

Another possibility is to reorganize the `expression` method and do some trickery with the grammar. I'm not a big fan of this approach because it means we have to modify the expression parsing and I'd rather not do that. However, for those interested, I'll explain it here. The first thing to do is define the grammar for this situation:

```
symbol = identifier | number | '+' | '-' | '('
expression = symbol restOfExpression
stmt = symbol restOfExpression | symbol '=' expression
```

We first split `expression` into two parts, a leading symbol and the rest of the expression. The leading symbol can be whatever starts an expression, an identifier, a number etc. We then define a `stmt` to be either an assignment or an expression. The only problem here is that `stmt` cannot be parsed with just one lookahead so we need to left factor `stmt` which was described in section 6.5.2. If we left factor `stmt` we arrive at:

```
stmt = symbol stmt'
stmt' = restOfExpression | '=' expression
```

In code this would be implemented as:

```
procedure stmt;
begin
    symbol();
    stmtPrime();
end;

procedure stmtPrime;
begin
  if sc.token = '=' then
    begin
    sc.nextToken;
    expression();
    end
  else
    restOfExpression;
end;
```

A third approach is to allow the parser to lookahead two tokens specifically for dealing with the assignment problem. This is easier than you might think and is going to be the solution we'll use. It means that the existing expression syntax and code is unchanged. This is useful in another sense because when parsing source code from files we won't be supporting interactive use and we can confine the need to respond to assignments and expressions to the interactive prompt.

Another possible solution is to employ a special keyword in front of the assignment, something like let a = 2. There is no longer any ambiguity in what is an assignment and what is an expression. Finally, we could solve the problem if we were to insist that to output the value of a symbol or expression we have to use a print statement, for example:

```
>>a = 2*7
>>print (a)
```

Again we have removed the ambiguity between an assignment and requesting output. As tempting as this is, most interpreters allow a user to access a value of an expression simply by typing the expression at the keyboard without any need for a print statement. I'd like to emulate similar functionality.

As we develop the language there will be further complications. In particular, we'll eventually have to deal with assignments such as:

a[2] = 4.5

that is indexable variables. We'll consider the syntax for such expressions in Chapter 9 but for interactive use, we'll wait until part 2.

How do we go about implementing deeper lookahead? Probably the easiest thing to do is to modify the lexical analyzer. We will add a new method to the lexical analyzer called pushBackToken. This will take a token as an argument. Its purpose is to push the token back into the lexical analyzer so that next time the method nextToken is called, it will retrieve the pushed back token. We can generalize this by allowing any number of tokens to be pushed back. We have to be careful about the order in which token will be retrieved, i.e., the first token pushed back should be the first to be retrieved. The way to do this is to use a queue. Figure 8.1 shows a queue that stores tokens. Just like a real queue of people, a queue has a place where data enters and a place where data leaves. The key property of a queue is that the first person (or data) to enter a queue is the first person to leave it. This is exactly the behavior we want with tokens. Two main operations can be applied to a queue, adding an item to the back of the queue called: to enqueue, and removing an item from the front of the queue, called dequeue.

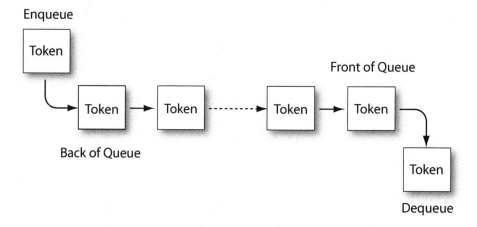

Figure 8.1 Operation of a token Queue.

What's this got to do with pushing back tokens? Assume we need to lookahead three tokens, this means we call nextToken three times and retrieve in order, token1, token2, and token3. We now want to push them back into the lexical analyzer. To push them back we need to push them in the order we retrieved them, token1, token2, and token3. Because the underlying data structure is a queue, we know that the next time we call nextToken, we will first retrieve token1 followed by token 2, and 3 which is exactly what we want.

8.2   Using a Queue for Lookahead

Before we make changes to the lexical analyzer, let's look at how we might use this to parse an assignment. We'll create two new methods, statement and assignment. statement is shown below.

```
procedure TSyntaxAnalysis.statement;
var token1, token2 : TTokenElement;
begin
  token1 := sc.tokenElement;
  sc.nextToken;
```

```
    token2 := sc.tokenElement;

  if sc.token = tEquals then
      begin
      if token1.FToken = tIdentifier then
         begin
         sc.nextToken;
         assignment (token1.FTokenString);
         end
      else
         raise ESyntaxException.Create('left-hand side of the
                  assignment must be a variable');
      end
  else
      begin
      sc.pushBackToken(token1);
      sc.pushBackToken(token2);
      sc.nextToken;
      writeln (expression:10:6);
      end;
end;
```

There are a couple of things going on here. The first thing we do is make copies of the current token as we enter the method, `token1` and the next token `token2` after calling `nextToken`. The current token could be an equals symbol if we've started parsing an assignment. If not, we push the two tokens, 1 and 2 back into the lexical stream and call `expression` as if nothing has happened.

If we do detect an equals symbol we move past that with another `nextToken` and call the assignment method. Before doing that we need to make sure that the first token, `token1` is a simple identifier. If it's not, then we issue an error. This is to safeguard against the user typing things like `23 = 5`.

One complication is that `expression` returns a double while `assignment` is just a statement and therefore has nothing to return. The easiest way to deal with this is to move the output of values into `statement`. In the case of `assignment` we print nothing whereas when we parse `expression` we write out the returned value.

The next thing to consider is the symbol table. For the simple calculator, this doesn't need to be very sophisticated, and we can use a dictionary to store all the symbols and their values. We'll create a new unit called `uSymbolTable.pas` and in that unit, we'll copy the following code:

```
unit uSymbolTable;

interface

Uses Generics.Collections;

type
```

```
  TSymbolTable =  TDictionary<string,double>;

  var symbolTable : TSymbolTable;

implementation

initialization
  symbolTable := TSymbolTable.Create;
finalization
  symbolTable.Free;
end.
```

We defined a new type TSymbolTable which is of type TDictionary with string type as
the key and a double as the corresponding value. We declare a global variable symbolTable
to be of type TSymbolTable. For convenience, I added an initialization and finalization section which will create and destroy the symbol table at startup and shutdown respectively.
And that's it for the symbol table. I said it wouldn't be very complicated.

8.3   Updating factor

In this section we'll update factor to deal with symbols in an expression and the method
for assignment. The updated factor method is given below:

```
function TSyntaxAnalysis.factor : double;
begin
  case sc.token of
    tInteger      : begin sc.nextToken; result := sc.tokenInteger; end;
    tFloat        : begin sc.nextToken; result := sc.tokenFloat; end;
    tIdentifier   : result := getIdentifierValue (sc.tokenString);
    tLeftParenthesis :
        begin
        sc.nextToken;
        result := expression;
        expect (tRightParenthesis);
        end;
  else
      raise ESyntaxException.Create('expecting scalar or left parentheses');
  end;
end;
```

This will modify the grammar for the factor production rule to:

factor = '(' expression ')' | number | variableSymbol

We have a new terminal called variableSymbol. This will have a token type of tIdentifier
with the string component stored in tokenString. In the factor method I've added a new
selection for tIdentifier. This calls a new method called getIdentifierValue. The

code isn't very long for this method but I didn't want to clutter up `factor`. The code is shown below:

```
function TSyntaxAnalysis.getIdentifierValue (const name : string) : double;
begin
   sc.nextToken;
   if symbolTable.ContainsKey (name) then
      result := symbolTable.items[name]
   else
      raise ESyntaxException.Create('symbol: "' + name + '" has no assigned value');
end;
```

`getIdentifierValue` takes an argument which is the string value for the `tIdentifier` token. Therefore on entry to `getIdentifierValue` we have the name of the symbol. Because this is a simple calculator we can be sure that the only thing the `tIdentifier` could be is a symbol name. It's not going to be the name of the sine function for example. We can therefore immediately check to see if the symbol name is already in the symbol table and if it is we retrieve the value for the symbol and return it. If the symbol name isn't in the symbol table, then this is an error because the user has tried to access a non-existent symbol. That's all we have to do with `factor`.

The last method is `assignment` which is shown below:

```
procedure TSyntaxAnalysis.assignment (const variableName : string);
var value : double;
begin
   value := expression;
   if symbolTable.containsKey (variableName) then
      symbolTable.AddOrSetValue (variableName, value)
   else
      symbolTable.Add (variableName, value);
end;
```

On entry to `assignment` we've already jumped over the equal symbol so we can straight-away parse an expression. This will evaluate the expression and return its value. `assignment` takes an argument which is the name of the symbol we detected on the left-hand side and we use this name to check if it is already in the dictionary or not. If it is in the dictionary we assign the value that came from `expression` to the symbol entry, otherwise, we create a new symbol and copy the value to the new symbol.

8.4 Updating the Lexical Analyzer

The final thing to do is update the lexical analyzer. We first declare a private variable in `TScanner` for the Queue called `tokenQueue`:

```
tokenQueue : TQueue<TTokenElement>;
```

In the TScanner constructor and destructor we'll create and destroy and Queue variable as
shown below:

```
constructor TScanner.Create;
begin
  inherited Create;
  addKeyWords;
  // Use to push tokens back into the stream
  tokenQueue := TQueue<TTokenElement>.Create;
end;

destructor TScanner.Destroy;
begin
  FKeyWordList.Free;
  // FStreamReader owns stream so stream will be freed too.
  freeAndNil(FStreamReader);
  tokenQueue.Free;
  inherited Destroy;
end;
```

In nextToken we'll add the following statements to the very beginning of the method:

```
  if tokenQueue.Count > 0 then
    begin
    FTokenElement := tokenQueue.Dequeue;
    exit;
    end;
```

We check if there are items in the queue. If there are we dequeue an item and copy it to the
token element variable and exit. If the queue is empty, we continue as before and fetch a
new token. The last thing is to add the method pushBackToken shown below:

```
procedure TScanner.pushBackToken (token : TTokenElement);
begin
  tokenQueue.Enqueue(token);
end;
```

This is a one-liner that takes a token as an argument, specifically a TTokenElement and
enqueues it (adds it) to the tokenQueue. I also added a property to TScanner to allow a
user to get access to the tokenElement after they've called nextToken:

```
property  tokenElement : TTokenElement read FTokenElement;
```

That completes the calculator for Part 1 of the series. Let's try running the new calculator:

```
Welcome to Rhodus Recognizer Console, Version 1.0
Data and Time: 12/8/2018, 4:50:47 PM
>> a = 2.3
>> b = 5.5
>> a+b
  7.800000
>> pi = 3.1415
>> radius = 5
>> area = pi*radius^2
>> area
 78.537500
>> circumference
Error: symbol: "circumference" has no assigned value
>>
```

Note the exception at the end when we try to display a symbol its never seen before. Seems to work. I'm not going to test this version of the calculator because in Part 2 we're going to take a very different direction and start implementing a virtual machine which will run programs generated by a code generator that will run downstream of the parser.

Exercise:

In the current version, when we assign pi to a value it can of course be overwritten later on. For example:

```
Welcome to Rhodus Recognizer Console, Version 1.0
Data and Time: 12/8/2018, 4:50:47 PM
>> pi = 3.1415
>> pi
3.1415
>> pi = 1
>> pi
1
>>
```

Update the code so that the calculator supports built-in read-only constants such as pi. For example if a user tries to assign a new value to pi they should receive the following error:

```
Welcome to Rhodus Calculator Console, Version 1.0
Data and Time: 12/8/2018, 4:50:47 PM
>> pi = 1
Error: pi is a built-in constant, you cannot redefine it
>>
```

9

Building a Recognizer

9.1 Introduction

We're going to wrap-up Part 1 by creating a recognizer for the Rhodus language version one. This will verify that a given source code is grammatically correct. We won't be generating an abstract syntax tree at this stage; this will be reserved for Part 2 of the series.[1]

In Chapter 6 and 8 we already created a syntax analyzer for expressions. Creating a syntax analyzer for the remainder of the grammar shouldn't be difficult if we use recursive descent.

Let's recall the full syntax specification for Rhodus version one that was given in Chapter 6:

```
mainProgram     = statementList [ ';' ] endOfStream
statementList   = statement { ; statement }
statement       = assignment | forStatement | ifStatement
                      | whileStatement | repeatStatement
                      | returnStatment | breakStatement
                      | function | endOfStream
variable        = simpleVariable | indexVariable
list            = '{' [ expressionList ] '}'
simpleVariable  = identifier
indexVariable   = identifier '[' expressionList ']'
expressionList  = expression { ',' expression }
assignment      = variable '=' expression
function        = FUNCTION identifier '(' [ argumentList ] ')' functionBody
functionBody    = statementList END
argumentList    = argument { ',' argument }
```

---

[1]The code for this chapter can be found in GitHub in the Calculator_Chapr9 folder.

```
argument          = identifier | REF variable
returnStatement   = RETURN expression
breakStatement    = BREAK
expression        = simpleExpression | simpleExpression relationalOp simpleExpression
simpleExpression  = term { addingOp term }
term              = factor { multiplyOp factor }
power             = { '+' | '-'} factor [ '^' power ]
factor            = '(' expression ')' | variable | number | string |
                        NOT factor | list | functionCall
functionCall      = identifier '(' [ expressionList ] ')'
addingOp          = '+' | '-' | OR | XOR
multiplyOp        = '*' | '/' | AND | MOD | DIV
relationalOp      = '==' | '!=' | '<' | '<=' | '>=' | '>'
whileStatement    = WHILE expression DO statementList END
repeatStatement   = REPEAT statementList UNTIL expression
forStatement      = FOR identifier = forList DO statementList END
forList           = value TO value | value DOWNTO value
ifStatement       = IF expression THEN statementList ifEnd
ifEnd             = END | ELSE statementList END
```

9.2   Syntax Specification

Let's take a more detailed look at the syntax specification. We begin with the start symbol, mainProgram. This is a list of statements with an optional semicolon and a final terminating endOfStream. Why make the semicolon optional? The simple reason is to make it easier on the user. Since we're at the end of the program at this point, a semicolon is not strictly necessary. Whether a user includes a semicolon or not shouldn't matter, so we'll let them do either.

The second question is why use endOfStream to terminate the program? We could for example use 'end' to terminate the program. This would be consistent with the use of 'end' elsewhere. But we don't have a starting token, so there is no matching opening clause. We could use something like:

```
main
   a = 5;
   b = 6;
end
```

This would be consistent with the rest of the language. In the end, I didn't want to clutter up the code further and decided that a program should be as simple as the following:

```
   a = 5;
   b = 6
```

However why do we need a terminator such as endOfSteam anyway? The problem arises in the way a `statementList` is defined and how we parse the main program. Consider this way to define a program:

```
mainProgram    = statementList
statementList = statement { ';' statement }
```

Imagine a situation such as:

```
a = 5
b = 4
```

Note the missing semicolon from the first statement. Given the previous grammar, the `mainProgram` and `statementList` methods can be implemented as follows:

```
procedure mainProgram;
begin
  statementList;
end;

procedure statementList;
begin
   statement;
   while sc.token = tSemicolon do
      begin
      expect (tSemicolon);
      statement;
      end;
end;
```

Once the parser reads the first line by way of `statement`, it starts to look for a semicolon as a marker to start reading the second statement. However because there is no semicolon, the `statementList` method will exit and return to `mainProgram` at which point it exits the parser entirely. There is no suggestion there was an error when in fact the entire second statement was missed. One way around this is to check for the `endOfStream` token in `mainProgram` so that we now write `mainProgram` as:

```
procedure mainProgram;
begin
  statementList;
  if sc.token <> tEndofStream then
     expect (tSemicolon);
end;
```

This time, as we exit `statementList`, we check whether we're at the end of the stream. If we're not then there must be additional code to parse, separated from the previous code with a semicolon. Hence we can check for a semicolon, and if one is missing, we report a syntax error. This resolves the problem we had.

Semicolons

Semicolons can sometimes be a contentious issue among programmers. Should we have
them or should we not? In Rhodus, the design is similar to Pascal where semicolons
separate statements. This, however, can result in some confusion for newcomers especially whether a semicolon should come after an `else` token. In the Rhodus grammar,
there is only one location where the semicolon is indicated, that is in the definition of
`statementList` which is repeated here:

```
statementList = statement { ; statement }
```

There is a key difference between C and Pascal-like languages with respect to the meaning
of the semicolon. In C and its derivatives, a semicolon is used to indicate the termination
of a statement. In Pascal-like languages, the semicolon is used to separate statements.
As eluded before, this has caused some confusion; for example, there is no need for a
semicolon after the `else` keyword because `else` is not at the end of a statement. Also,
there is no need for a semicolon at the end of the last statement in a block because there is
usually already a terminator such as end. See the Pascal below fragment for an example:

```
if a > 5 then
   begin
   x = 5.6;
   y = x * 2 // No semicolon here
   end;
```

It's human nature that mistakes will be made and a common mistake is in placing the
semicolon. As a result, some Pascal compilers will ignore any unnecessary semicolon
before an end keyword. In Rhodus, we will implement similar behavior. For example, we
will allow the following two code fragments to be legal:

```
if a > 5 then        if a > 5 then
   x = 5.6;              x = 5.6;
   y = x + 2            y = x + 2;
end                  end
```

Every language designer will have to make small decisions like this, and to a purist, they
may be unacceptable. It might be possible to modify the grammar to accommodate these
changes, but we won't attempt that here.

statementList

A statement list is a statement followed by zero or more semicolons followed by another
statement. This is a straightforward production rule to implement. The key identification
token is the semicolon. As mentioned above it does mean that a statement just before an
identification token such as end or `until` won't need a semicolon. As we also mentioned
before, this is likely to cause some frustration for new users because out of habit they

will likely include a semicolon resulting in an error. To help the user, we'll make the semicolon on the penultimate statement optional. To implement this we only have to add an `if` statement in `statementList` that checks for an end like keyword, which will include `until`, `end`, and `else`.

```
// statementList = statement { ; statement }
procedure TSyntaxAnalysis.statementList;
begin
   statement;
   while sc.token = tSemicolon do
      begin
      expect (tSemicolon);
      if sc.token in [tUntil, tEnd, tElse, tEndOfStream] then
         break;
      statement;
      end;
end;
```

We also include `endOfStream` in the closing list because this will also avoid a missing token error on the very last statement in the program.

9.3 Specific Examples

Here are some specific examples of recursive descent code for dealing with the Rhodus grammar. Because we're just writing a recognizer, the methods won't return any information back to the caller such as a subtree for building the abstract syntax tree.

Statement

`statement` is implemented as a `case` switch and will attempt to identify one of ten possible tokens. If it can't identify any, this is a syntax error. Note that the `println` token is included here as well. The tenth case option is `tEndOfStream`. The reason this is here is to take care of empty files. For example, a file that just contains a comment will only return the `tEndOfStream` token and we need to make sure we don't get a missing statement syntax error.

```
// statement = assignment | forStatement | ifStatement
//                 | whileStatement | repeatStatement
//                 | returnStatment | breakStatement | endOfStream
function  TSyntaxAnalysis.statement : TASTNode;
begin
  case sc.token of
     tIdentifier: result := assignment;
     tIf         : result := ifStatement;
     tFor        : result := forStatement;
     tWhile      : result := whileStatement;
```

```
      tRepeat    : result := repeatStatement;
      tReturn    : result := returnStmt;
      tBreak     : result := breakStmt;
      tFunction  : functionDef;
      tPrintln   : printlnStatement;
   tEndOfStream : exit;
  else
     raise ESyntaxException.Create('expecting assignment, if,
                 for, while or repeat statement');
  end;
end;
```

9.3.1 Indexed variables

Version one of Rhodus supports indexed variables to access elements in lists or strings. For example:

```
a = {1,2,3,4};
a[1] = 3.4;
x = a[1] + a[2];
s = "Hello"
s[3] = "g"
```

To support this the grammar defines a variable as:

```
variable = simpleVariable | indexedVariable
```

A simple variable is just an identifier, such as x. The indexed variable is defined by the production rule:

```
indexedVariable = identifier '[' expressionList ']'
```

and expressionList in turn is defined as:

```
expressionList = expression { ',' expression }
```

The use of repetition in the expressionList means that we allow indexing of the form:

```
a[1,3,4]
```

Note that the indexed elements themselves can be expressions so that we can also write:

```
a[i+j, k*2]
```

The only caveat is that the expressions must resolve to an integer type. We can't test for this in the syntax phase; we also can't deal with it at the semantic stage because Rhodus is not strongly typed and it is only at runtime that we know what the type will be for a given variable.

To support indexing, the first thing we do is modify the assignment method:

```
// assignment = variable '=' expression
procedure  TSyntaxAnalysis.assignment;
```

```
begin
  expect (tIdentifier);
  if sc.token = tLeftBracket then
    begin
    sc.nextToken;
    expressionList;
    expect (tRightBracket);
    end;

  expect (tEquals);
  expression;
end;
```

The code starts by expecting an identifier. If we next find a square bracket we proceed by invoking the method `expressionList` to handle the list of indices. This method is shown below.

It is worth pointing out that we are not dealing with the situation we had in Chapter 8 where a user was able to type an assignment or an expression at the interactive prompt. The code we describe here is for parsing source code found in files. For interactive use we'll have to modify the `assignment` method as we did in Chapter 8. This will be described in Part 2.

```
// argumentList = expression { ',' expression }
procedure  TSyntaxAnalysis.expressionList;
begin
  expression;
  while sc.token = tComma do
    begin
    sc.nextToken;
    expression;
    end;
end;
```

We've seen the pattern before in `expressionList` where we use a while loop to check for the delimiter, in this case, a comma. If there is no delimiter, we assume we've reached the end and return to `assignment` and check for the closing square bracket.

The other big change is in `factor` where we must deal with indexed variables on the right-hand side of an expression. The new `factor` method is shown below. The main change is when we spot an identifier, we also check for a left square bracket. If one is found we call `expressionList` then close with a check for a right square bracket. That's all there is to do with indexing.

```
// factor = integer | float | '(' expression ')'
procedure TSyntaxAnalysis.factor;
var ch : char;
begin
  case sc.token of
    tInteger       : sc.nextToken;
```

```
    tFloat          : sc.nextToken;
    tIdentifier   :
          begin
          sc.nextToken;
          case sc.token of
             tLeftBracket :
                 begin
                 sc.nextToken;
                 expressionList;
                 expect (tRightBracket);
                 end;
          end;
          end;
    tLeftParenthesis :
          begin
          sc.nextToken;
          expression;
          expect (tRightParenthesis);
          end;
  else
     raise ESyntaxException.Create('expecting scalar,
         identifier or left parentheses');
  end;
end;
```

You may be wondering why I've used a case statement to detect the square bracket. This is because when we come to describe user-defined functions, we also need to support the syntax for calling functions, such as:

```
x = add (3,4)
```

9.3.2 Looping

Of the looping constructs, the repeat statement is the simplest to implement and is shown below. Note that we must call nextToken first in order to get past the repeat token. After that we expect a list of statements followed by the until token and an expression.

```
// repeatStatement = REPEAT statementList UNTIL expression
procedure  TSyntaxAnalysis.repeatStatement;
begin
  sc.nextToken;
  statementList;
  expect (tUntil);
  expression;
end;
```

The while loop is equally straightforward:

```
// whileStatement = WHILE expression DO statementList END
procedure  TSyntaxAnalysis.whileStatement;
begin
  sc.nextToken;
  expression;
  expect (tDo);
  statementList;
  expect (tEnd);
end;
```

The `for` loop is a bit longer because we have to parse the looping syntax:

```
// forStatement = FOR identifier = expression
// TO/DOWNTO expression DO statementList END
procedure  TSyntaxAnalysis.forStatement;
begin
  sc.nextToken;
  expect (tIdentifier);
  expect (tEquals);
  expression;
  if sc.token in [tTo, tDownTo] then
     begin
     expect (tTo);
     expression;
     expect (tDo);
     statementList;
     expect (tEnd);
     end
  else
     raise ESyntaxException.Create('expecting "to" or "downto" in for loop');
end;
```

The only one complication is we need to check for `to` as well as `downto`.

Each looping construct can unconditionally exit using the `break` statement. The code for this is just one line to advance the token.

```
procedure TSyntaxAnalysis.breakStmt;
begin
  sc.nextToken;
end;
```

9.3.3 Conditional statements

The conditional grammar is more complicated but not difficult to implement. We avoid the problem of the dangling else by insisting on every `if` statement being terminated with an end token. We might revisit this in Part 2 to show how we could also use `elseif` which has some advantages. We split the `if` code in two to match the grammar, `ifStatment` and `ifEnd`:

```
// ifStatement = IF expression THEN statement ifEnd
procedure  TSyntaxAnalysis.ifStatement;
begin
  sc.nextToken;
  expression;
  expect (tThen);
  statementList;
  ifEnd;
end;

// ifEnd = END | ELSE statementList END
procedure  TSyntaxAnalysis.ifEnd;
begin
  if sc.token = tElse then
     begin
     sc.nextToken;
     statementList;
     expect (tEnd);
     end
  else
     expect (tEnd);
end;
```

In ifEnd we check for the else. If no else is found we expect an end token, otherwise
we deal with the else clause.

9.3.4   User defined functions

We have to decide how functions are called since there are two alternatives. For example,
assume we have a user-defined function called helloWorld. How should this be called?
Like this hellowWorld; or this helloWorld()? If we intend to support the passing of
functions to user-defined functions, then we need some way to specify a function variable.
The simplest way to do this is to define a user-defined function without brackets as a reference to the function. A function with brackets means the function is called. For example,
consider the code:

```
// Define a function
function myfunc
  return 5
end;

// Pass the function as an argument
function callfunc (func)
    return func()
end;

// Pass the function reference
callfunc (myfunc);
```

```
// Or call the function
x = myfunc();
```

In the example we define a user function `myfunc`. We can either call this function by using `myfunc()` which will return the integer 5, or pass a reference to the `callfunc` function using `myfunc`. If we tried to pass `myfunc()` it would actually pass 5 to `callfunc` which is not what we intended.

Function calls can have no arguments so that we define a function call as follows:

`functionCall = identifier '(' [ expressionList ] ')'`

where the `expressionList` is optional. This allows use to write the following legal code:

```
function helloWorld
   return "Hello World"
end
```

Syntax checking for user defined functions is straightforward and is shown below:

```
// function = function identifier [ '(' argumentList ')' ]
procedure  TSyntaxAnalysis.functionDef;
begin
  sc.nextToken;
  expect (tIdentifier);
  if sc.token = tLeftParenthesis then
     begin
     sc.nextToken;
     argumentList;
     expect (tRightParenthesis);
     end;
  statementList;
  expect (tEnd);
end;
```

The `argumentList` is a separate production and takes care of the comma separated argument list (if present) and the special case where an argument is passed by reference:

```
// argumentList = argument { ',' argument }
procedure  TSyntaxAnalysis.argumentList;
begin
  argument;
  while sc.token = tComma do
     begin
     sc.nextToken;
     argument;
     end;
end;

// argument = identifier | REF identifier
```

```
procedure  TSyntaxAnalysis.argument;
begin
  if sc.token = tRef then
    sc.nextToken;
  expect (tIdentifier);
end;
```

The final aspect to consider is when a function is called. This is dealt with in the `factor` method. We'd already set this up in anticipation for function calls by using a case statement after we detected an identifier. The code below shows how to augment the case statement to handle user function calls:

```
tIdentifier :
    begin
    sc.nextToken;
    case sc.token of
        // Check for function call, eg add (a,b)
      tLeftParenthesis :
        begin
        sc.nextToken;
        if sc.token <> tRightParenthesis then
            expressionList;
        expect (tRightParenthesis);
        end;
        // Check for indexed variable, eg x[i]
      tLeftBracket :
        begin
        sc.nextToken;
        expressionList;
        expect (tRightBracket);
        end;
    end;
    end;
```

9.3.5   Miscellaneous operators

We need to finish off `factor` because we're currently not dealing with strings, the Boolean `NOT` and `True` and `False`. Also, we need to handle the list data type. The first of these is very straightforward and is given in the code below:

```
tString :
    begin
    sc.nextToken;
    end;
tNOT :
    begin
    sc.nextToken;
    expression;
```

```
        end;
    tFalse :
        begin
        sc.nextToken;
        end;
    tTrue :
        begin
        sc.nextToken;
        end;
```

Handling the list is only a little bit more involved and means detecting the curly bracket:

```
    tLeftCurleyBracket :
        begin
        sc.nextToken;
        if sc.token <> tRightCurleyBracket then
            doList;
        expect (tRightCurleyBracket);
        end;
```

We need to account for the situation where the user specifies an empty list such as: x = {}. If the list is not empty we call the method doList which is shown below:

```
procedure TSyntaxAnalysis.doList;
begin
  expression;
  while sc.token = tComma do
    begin
    sc.nextToken;
    expression;
    end;
end;
```

There isn't much to this method, but one thing to note is that it is recursive. For each element in the list, it calls expression. It is possible that expression includes other lists. This allows us to parse arbitrarily deep nestings in a list. For something that at first glance might have been difficult to parse, lists turn out to be remarkably simple to parse.

Missing Operators

Another thing thing we need to do is add the missing arithmetic operators such as div and mod to term, and the Boolean operators and and or, xor to term and simpleExpression respectively. Finally we renamed the original expression to simpleExpression and reserved expression to handle the comparison operators. There isn't much to the new expression method but is shown below for completeness:

```
// expression = simpleExpression | simpleExpression relationalOp simpleExpression
procedure  TSyntaxAnalysis.expression;
```

```
begin
  simpleExpression;
  while sc.token in [tLessThan, tLessThanOrEqual, tMoreThan,
            tMoreThanOrEqual, tNotEqual, tEquivalence] do
    begin
    sc.nextToken;
    simpleExpression;
    end;
end;
```

9.4 Conclusion

That completes the description of the recognizer. We don't do any formal testing here but will leave that to Part 2. However, a number of test scripts were written to shake out the most obvious bugs (See Appendix). The following are a few examples of source code that can be successfully parsed by the recognizer.

```
// Removes spaces from a string
oldStr = "A str ing"; newStr = "";
for i = 0 to 8 do
    if oldStr[i] != ' ' then
        newStr = newStr + oldStr[i]
    end
end
```

```
// Repeat a string (text) count times
function repeatString(count, text)
   ret = "";

   for i = 1 To count do
      ret = ret + text
   end;
   return ret;
end;

println (repeatString(5, "ha"))
```

```
// Compute Hamming Number (from rosettacode.org)
function hamming (limit)
   h[0] = 1;
   x2 = 2; x3 = 3; x5 = 5;
   i  = 0; j  = 0; k = 0;
   for n = 1 to limit do
       h[n] = min(x2, min(x3, x5));
       if x2 == h[n] then i = i + 1; x2 = 2*h[i] end;
       if x3 == h[n] then j = j + 1; x3 = 3*h[j] end;
```

Command	Description
run fileName	Loads source code from a file and runs the code
edit fileName	Load the file into notepad for editing
list fileName	Display the contents of the file to the console
dir	Lists all files with the extension .rh
quit	Quit the application

Table 9.1 REPL Commands

```
        if x5 == h[n] then k = k + 1; x5 = 5*h[k] end;
    end;
    return h[limit -1];
end;

// We have to initialize lists this way because
// we don't yet have any specific list support
h = {0,0,0,0,0,0,0,0,0,0,0,0,0};

for i = 1 to 20 do
    println (hamming (i));
end
```

9.5 Updates to the REPL

As a final flourish I decided to update the REPL to make it easier to do interactive tests. In the previous REPL it was possible to type quit to exit the REPL. I decided to add to this four new commands. These include, run, edit, list and dir (See Table 9.1).

There is nothing at all special about the new REPL code and I didn't want to spend too much time on it because we're going to revisit the REPL in much more detail in Part 2. I created a simple function that would run the commands, list, dir or edit. This is shown below together with a helper routine getSampleScriptsDir:

```
function getSampleScriptsDir : string;
begin
   result := TDirectory.GetParent(TDirectory.GetParent(getCurrentDir))
                + '\SampleScripts';
end;

function runCommand (const src : string) : boolean;
var fileName, sdir : string;
begin
   sdir := getSampleScriptsDir + '\';
```

```
      result := False;
      if leftStr (src, 4) = 'list' then
         begin
         fileName := trim (rightStr (src, length (src) - 4));
         if TFile.Exists (sdir + fileName) then
            writeln (TFile.ReadAllText(sdir + fileName))
         else
            writeln ('No such file');
         result := True;
         end;
      if leftStr (src, 4) = 'edit' then
         begin
         fileName := trim (rightStr (src, length (src) - 4));
         ShellExecute(0, nil, PChar('notepad.exe'),
            PChar(sdir + '\' + fileName), nil, SW_SHOWNORMAL);
         result := True;
         end;
      if src = 'dir' then
         begin
         for fileName in TDirectory.GetFiles(sdir, '*.rh') do
            writeln (extractFileName (sdir + fileName));
         result := True;
      end;
end;
```

I store the test scripts in `sampleScript` on the same level as `Win32` in the project group. Since the current directory is at `.\Win32\Debug` I need to get the parent of the parent of the current directory and then subdirectory to `sampleScripts`. As a result, I preface every file access with `sampleScripts`.

There are hardwired constants in this code which is never a good thing to do but as I said this is a temporary hack. In future we'll probably us a dictionary where the dictionary value points to a command method.

`runCommand` checks for the specific command and runs the appropriate code. For `edit` we call the external editor notepad since we can be confident that notepad will be available on the host computer. For both `list` and `dir` I make use of the `IOUtils` class which has a range of very useful functions which makes the code quite short. This includes reading all text from a file and listing all files in a directory, as well as finding the parent of a directory.

The other function is `runCode` which when given source code, will invoke the interpreter and report any errors it finds. This code is shown below:

```
procedure runCode (const src : string);
begin
   sc.scanString(src);
   try
      sc.nextToken;
      sy.mainProgram;
      writeln ('Success');
```

```
     except
        on e:exception do
           writeln ('Error: ' + e.Message + ' at line number '
                   + inttostr (sc.tokenElement.lineNumber) + ' column: '
                   + inttostr (sc.tokenElement.columnNumber));
     end;
end;
```

Finally, some changes were made to the main program. We look for three situations, running one of the commands dir, list, or edit, running the command run or if no command is entered we pass the input text directly to the interpreter. The code that was changed is shown below:

```
        try
          displayPrompt;
          readln (sourceCode);
          if sourceCode = 'quit' then
             break;
          if leftStr (sourceCode, 3) = 'run' then
             begin
             fileName := trim (rightStr (sourceCode, length (sourceCode) - 3));
             if TFile.Exists (fileName) then
                begin
                runCode (TFile.ReadAllText(fileName));
                continue;
                end
             else
                begin
                writeln ('File not found');
                continue;
                end;
             end
          else
             if runCommand (sourceCode) then
                continue;

          if sourceCode <> '' then
             runCode (sourceCode);
        except
          on e:exception do
             writeln (e.Message);
```

Again, this is not a permanent solution for the REPL, it's just temporary until we come up with a design that incorporates name completion and some help support. The danger is that temporary solutions can turn into permanent solutions. We must be careful not to build on this REPL but to rewrite it in Part 2.

Appendix: Test Scripts

The following scripts were used to shake out the most obvious bugs from the recognizer. We will wait until Part 2 before we do more thorough testing.

```
// Simple for loop
for i = 1 to 10 do
    a = 5;
    b = 8
end;

// ------------------------------
// Nested for loop
for i = 0 to 10 do
    a = 5;
    for j = 0 to 20 do
        b = 7;
        for k = 0 to 30 do
            c = 9
        end
    end;
    println ("Hello");
end;

// ------------------------------
// Nested for loop with indexing
nRows = 10;
nCols = 10;
for i = 0 to nRows - 1 do
    for j = 0 to nCols - 1 do
        matrix[i,j] = 3.1415;
    end
end;

// ------------------------------
// Simple User defined function
function sayHello
    println ("Say Hello")
end;

// ------------------------------
// User defined function
function mean (a, b, c, d)
    sum = a + b + c + d;
    return sum/4
end;
```

```
x = mean (2,3,4,5);
println (x);


// -----------------------------
// Simple if statement
if a < 5 then
   b = 6
end;

// -----------------------------
// if statement with else clause
if a > 6 then
   b = 9
else
   x = 7
end;

// -----------------------------
// Nested if statements
if a > 6 then
   b = 9
else
   if b < 3 then
      x = 7
   else
      x = 8
   end
end;

// -----------------------------
// Lists
a = {1,2,3,4};
a = {1,2,{3,4}};
a = {1,2,{3,{4,5}}};
a = {"Hello", 3, False, {True, False}};

// -----------------------------
// Repeat statement
repeat
   a = 10
until a < 5;

// -----------------------------
// while statement
while a < b do
    a = 6;
    b = 10;
```

```
end;

// -------------------------------
// while with comparison operators
while (a < b) and (c >= 6) do
    a = 6;
    b = 10;
end;

// -------------------------------
// Boolean operations
x = not False;
x = False and True;
x = False or True;
x = not (False or True);
x = False xor True and True;
x = y1 < y2 and x1 > x2;
x = y1 >= y2 and not (y3 <= y4);
x = (y1 != 6);
x = y1 == 6;

// -------------------------------
// Arithmetic and string operations
x = 5; y = 7;
z = x + y; z = x - y;    z = x*y; z = x/y;
z = x^y;    z = y div x; z = y mod x;

s1 = "Say"; s2 = " "; s3 = "Hello";
s4 = s1 + s2 + s3;

// -------------------------------
// Empty file, just comments
/* A multiline
comment */

// -------------------------------
// Test correct line number when there is an error
println ("Test comment line increment");
x = 1;
// Comment
x = 2
x = 3;   // <--- Line 5
x = 5;
// An error should be reported at line 5, column 1
```

EBNF

EBNF is a language for describing syntax. The acronym stands for Extended Backus-Naur Form. It is an extended version of an older effort called BNF, or Backus-Naur form. EBNF was developed to overcome some readability limitations of BNF. Any EBNF specification can be expressed in BNF but the resulting BNF specification will be more verbose. EBNF also tends to make it easier to specify grammars that can be parsed using recursive descent.

EBNF describes syntax using a series of production rules that includes terminal and non-terminal symbols. Non-terminal symbols are higher level constructs within a language. For example, an assignment, a function, an expression and ultimately the entire program itself. The terminals are the most elementary tokens defined in a language and will include things such as integers, identifiers, plus, minus etc. A production rule in EBNF has a left and right side separated by a definition symbol, =. Here is a simple production rule:

A = B C

It is read as A is defined as B followed by C. A real example of a real production rule would be:

```
assignment = identifier '=' value
```

That is an assignment is defined as an identifier, followed by a '=', followed by a value. The intent is that any non-terminal symbols on the right-hand side will have their own production rules. Terminal symbols such as '=' will not.

According to the standard, terminals are depicted in lower case and non-terminals in upper-case. In addition, terminals that represent themselves, for example, the equal symbol can be given in quotes. Moreover, both non-terminals and terminals can be represented with

Usage	Notation
definition	=
alternation	|
repetition	{ ... }
optional	[..]
grouping	(...)

Table A.1 A summary some of the notation used in EBNF.

full names, usually lower case in order to make their meaning clearer. The assignment production rule above follows these conventions. The EBNF standard also states that the end of a production should be terminated with a semicolon, we don't use that here. Many of these conventions are described in the ISO/IEC 14977:1996 Information technology – Syntactic metalanguage – Extended BNF (https://www.iso.org/standard/26153.html).

Not everyone, of course, adheres to the standard and there are a number of variants and modification used in the literature. For example the definition symbol, '=' is sometimes represented using '::=' and was used in the original BNF proposal. Sometimes repetition is indicated using an asterisk after a group that should be repeated, for example, ('+' term)*. This also happens to be the convention used in specifying a repeated element in a regular expression. We use the ISO standard in this book except for the terminating semicolon which we will omit.

A series of production rules is used to describe a complete language. For example, we might extend the `assignment` rule with:

```
assignment = identifier '=' value
value      = integer | floating-point-number
```

Here we introduce a new notation, | that means OR. Therefore the production rule for value is read: 'A value is as an integer OR a floating-point-number'.

Every EBNF specification has a start symbol. For a programming language the start symbol will be the non-terminal often called `program` otherwise S is often used. A table that shows some of the symbols used in Table A.1.

Let's consider some examples. A number such as 1234 or -345 can be described using:

```
number = [ '-' ] digit { digit }
```

That is a number can start with an optional negative sign, followed by a digit then any number of digits. A identifier such as `count` or `count_6` would be described using:

```
identifier = letter { letter | digit }
```

If we allow an underscore to start an identifier we can modify the description to:

```
identifier = letter | underscore { letter | digit | underscore }
```

Repetition

Curly parentheses are used to indicate that something is repeated zero or more times. For example, the production rule below is a classic way to describe a comma-separated list:

```
argumentList = argument { ',' argument }
```

Here we see that comma argument is repeated between zero and more times.

Optional

Square brackets are used to indicate optional components in a production. For example:

```
term = [ '-' ] factor
```

Alternatives

Alternatives are indicated using the ' | ' line between the alternatives. For example:

```
digit = '0' | '1' | '2' | '3' | '4' | '5' | '6' | '7' | '8' | '9'
```

Grouping

Grouping can be used to eliminate alternatives. A common example is when indicating a plus or minus for an expression:

```
expr = expr ('+' | '-') expr
```

which can be combined with repetition to produce an LL(1) parsable grammar:

```
expr = term { ('+' | '-') term }
```

History

1. VERSION: 1.0

   Date: 2019-1-6

   Author(s): Herbert M. Sauro

   Title: Writing an Interpreter in Object Pascal

   Modification(s): First Public Release

2. VERSION: 1.01

   Date: 2019-1-14

   Author(s): Herbert M. Sauro

   Title: Writing an Interpreter in Object Pascal

   Modification(s): Went through the text again and fixed some errors in example Rhodus code. Also corrected a few minor typographical errors.

3. VERSION: 1.02

   Date: 2019-2-16

   Author(s): Herbert M. Sauro

   Title: Writing an Interpreter in Object Pascal

   Modification(s): For some reason in Chapter 3, I used TTokenRecord in the code snippets when I should have use FTokenRecord. This has been corrected. I also changed the variable name yyReader in the scanner to FStreamReader to be more consistent with Object Pascal variable naming. I also tidied up some inconsistent indenting in the code. I wish to thank JN for identifying these issues.

Index

Symbols

www.ingramcontent.com/pod-product-compliance
Lightning Source LLC
LaVergne TN
LVHW081527050326
832903LV00025B/1669